Mel Bay Presents

HOW TO CREATE AND DEVELOP A JAZZ SAX SOLO

By Arnie Berle

1 2 3 4 5 6 7 8 9 0

CONTENTS

PREFACE

What do I play? This is the most common question asked by the beginning jazz student when he is given a series of chord symbols and asked to improvise something. Even the "professional" jazz player asks himself the same question at sometime in his career. The purpose of this book is to try to help the student arrive at some answers to this complex question that touches at the very heart of musical creativity. While there is no explanation for that rare phenomenon of pure inspiration it is safe to say that even the most mature jazz performer has certain tools and devices which he resorts to in pre-composing his "spontaneous" solos. The most casual examination of a number of solos by any of the great jazz masters will reveal a repetoire of motives and phrases or patterns which occur over and over again through any number of his solos. This is not to imply that the master player repeats himself with every chorus or even every other chorus. Instead he will continualy find new ways to reshape, redefine, combine and alter and rephrase his well-practiced ideas. In this book we will explore some of the ways and techniques used by the great jazz masters so that you will have a better understanding of the techniques and devices involved in the creative process. In this way you will develop, stimulate and refine your own built in resevoir of creativity and be in a better position to know "what to play" when confronted with a set of chord changes.

INTRODUCTION

Before we get into the subject of the book it is important that the student have the following

1. A knowledge of all major and minor scales

2. A knowledge of major 7th, minor 7th, dominant 7th and diminished 7th chords.

3. The ability to read music.

If any of the above areas are not developed fully the student should make every effort to correct any weakness he may have. Otherwise his progress may be slowed down.

PRACTICING

There is no question that any student will only benefit from the material in this book in direct proportion to the amount of time he spends in thinking about the theoretical material and in practicing the written musical examples. All suggested assignments should be done in other keys in addition to the keys given in the assignment. It would be best if all assignments were done in all keys. As a writer I have had the opportunity to know many of the leading jazz artists of the world. You would be amazed to know the great amount of time these accomplished and gifted artists put into perfecting their skills. There are no short cuts and no luck involved. They are great because they worked as it.

IMPROVISATION

I think at this time we should have an understanding of just what improvisation is all about so that we know what our goals are. Simply defined, improvisation is the art of creating melodies over a given harmonic (chordal) framework or structure. If we could for a while, let's compare the studying of improvisation with studying a language. A persons ability to communicate either orally through conversation or visualy through the written word depends largely on the scope and understanding of his native language and the command he has of the vocabulary of that language. The better the command of the vocabulary, the better one is able to communicate his thoughts, desires and ideas. So too in music which is the universal language. The jazz player develops his vocabulary first by imitation of established sounds performed by established jazz artists but ultimately he must expand his vocabulary so that instead of merely copying some other persons vocabulary he can develop his own.

THE ELEMENTS OF JAZZ

Jazz like all music consists of three basic elements: melody, harmony, and rhythm. One more element which is characteristic to jazz but not to any other type of music may be called the jazz tone or jazz sound. An understanding of each of the essential elements will be a big help in learning how to create a decent jazz solo.

4

MELODY

Melody may be defined as an agreeable or pleasant succession of tones. A tune. The tones which make up a melody are derived from a group of related tones called a key.

HARMONY

Harmony is created by combining certain notes of a key into blocks of three or more notes called chords. These chords are then used to embellish or accompany a given melody.

RHYTHM

Rhythm may be defined as a regular, steady recurrance of beat. It is in this area of rhythm that the jazz player differs from the classical player. The jazz player does not always play exactly with the rhythmic pulse. He may play slightly ahead of the beat or slightly behind the beat. This feeling may vary from one player to another player. Just hearing a classical performer and a jazz performer play the same melodic line will reveal the difference in rhythmic concept.

JAZZ TONE

Another area which completely separates the classical performer from the jazz performer is in the area of tone or sound. While the classical musician strives for a certain pure or ideal sound on his instrument, the jazz musician prefers finding his own sound. The jazz player makes use of varying shades of vibrato. He uses lip slurs and bends and even growls. He also uses mutes to help project a particular sound. As in the area of rhythm the difference between a jazz artist and a classical artist can best be understood by simply listening to both artists playing the same piece of music. The difference in sound would be most obvious. See page 75.

MAJOR SCALE - DIATONIC 7th CHORDS-RELATED MODES

The basis of all jazz improvisation is the major scale, its seven diatonic seventh chords and their corresponding modes. An understanding of the relationship between chords and scales is absolutely essential in developing the principles of developing a jazz solo.

Chords come from scales. By taking the 1st, 3rd, 5th, and 7th notes from a particular scale we form the chord that is related to that scale. Every major scale contains within itself six other scales which are called MODES. By taking the 1st, 3rd, 5th, and 7th notes from any major scale and from each of the modes within that scale we form all of the chords which may be used to harmonize any melody based on that major scale.

Below is the C major scale shown with each of its derived modes and the chords related to each mode.

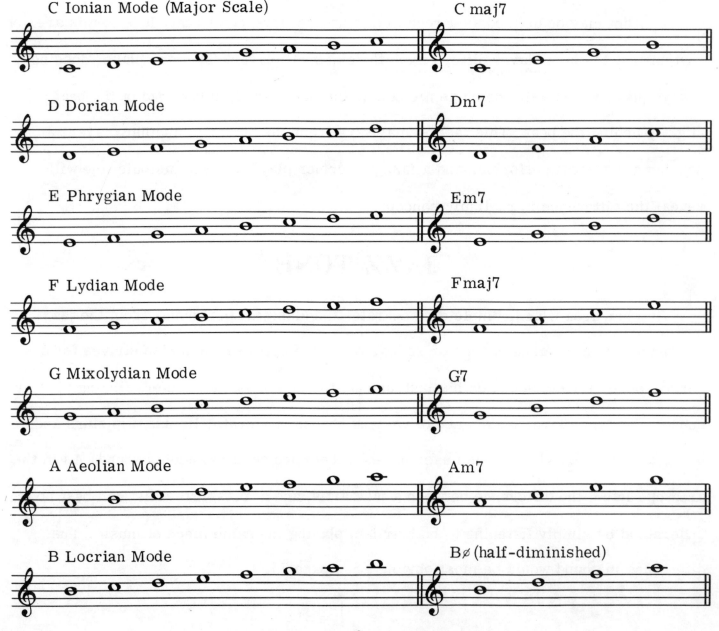

Below is an illustration showing the C major scale and all of the modes contained within that scale. Notice the major scale is called the ionian mode.

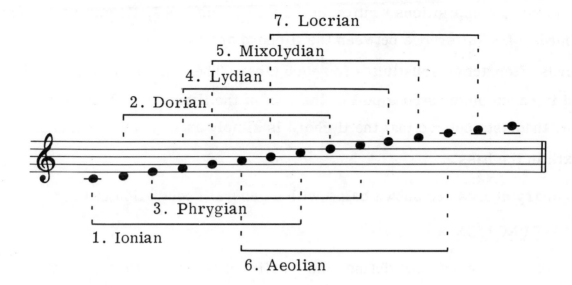

The chords which are formed from the C major scale and each of the modes within that scale are known as the "diatonic seventh chords". The notes which make up each chord come from the original major scale without any alterations such as sharps or flats which are not in the original scale.

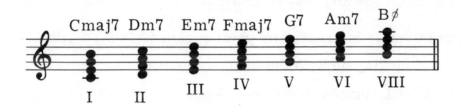

All chords within a particular key are identified by a Roman numeral.

THE QUALITY OF EACH CHORD REMAINS THE SAME IN ALL MAJOR KEYS.

CHORD QUALITY	CHORD SYMBOL
I and IV chords in all keys are major 7ths	Maj7
II, III, and VI chords in all keys are minor 7ths	m7
The V chord in all keys is a dominant 7th	7
The VII chord in all keys is a half-diminished	∅
and is also called a minor 7th b5	m7b5

THE PRIMARY CHORDS

In classical harmony the PRIMARY or chords of first importance are the I, IV, and V chords. However, compositions written in the jazz idiom use I, II, and V chords as the primary chords. The difference between the II chord and the IV chord are so slight that the two chords often act as substitutes for each other. The jazz players preferance for the II chord is based on the strong pull of the root of the II chord to the root of the V chord. Many theorists believe that the II chord is simply an inverted form of the IV chord with the sixth in the bass.

The primary chords are shown below with a general explanation of each.

CHORD	FUNCTION
I	It is the chord that defines the tonality of the key. It offers rest at the end of a series of chords. It is the point of resolution toward which all other chords move.
V	This chord sets up the tension which gives the progression a feeling of foward motion.
II	This chord usually is placed before the V chord. It delays and heightens the feeling of tension and foward motion.

Forward motion in music is created by placing chords in a position which best generates the feeling of moving on with the ultimate goal of resolving to the I chord. The series of chords which best creates this forward motion is the following progression.

II to V to I

Converting the roman numerals back into the key of C would give us the following progression. Dm7 - G7 - Cmaj7

The jazz musician in developing his solo immediately recognizes the above chord symbols as being the primary chords in the key of C and knows instantly that he must base his solo on the scales or modes or chords which are applicable to the key of C. As he plays through his solo he must recognize each new change of key by the primary chords of each new key and then instantly play on those scales, modes or chords which apply to the new key.

THE BLUES

Since jazz improvisation began with the first attempts at improvisation on the blues it is only right that any study of improvisation should also begin with the blues. The whole history of jazz may be traced through the various ways in which the blues have been treated in each of the different eras of jazz. From the earliest recordings of King Oliver with Louis Armstrong through every period which followed, the blues was the form most used by the leading jazz artists as the medium with which to express their musical statements. While the harmonic structure went through a number of different changes beginning with the earliest three chord blues progression to the little more advanced chords of the swing era to the most complex form of blues played in the bebop period and back to the more simpler form used by the rock players of the '50s, certain basic harmonic characteristics have remained unchanged. Below is an example of a basic blues progression.

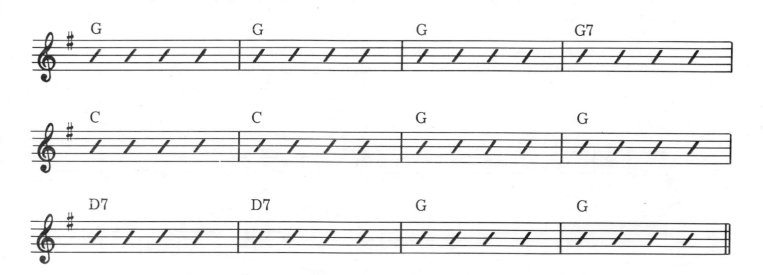

HARMONIC CHARACTERISTICS

The three basic harmonic characteristics which must be contained in all blues progressions no matter what period of jazz the players are involved in whether New Orleans style, Swing, Bebop or Rock are listed below.

1. The first four measures must begin with the tonic or I chord.

2. The second four measure phrase begins with a movement to the sub-dominant or the IV chord and then a return to the tonic by the seventh measure.

3. The third four measure phrase begins with a movement to the dominant or the V chord and then ending the phrase on the eleventh measure with a return to the I chord. The movement from the V to the I chord may either be direct as shown above or may go through the IV chord as V-IV-I (D7-C7-G). As you go through the book you will see a number of different examples of blues progressions.

MELODIC CHARACTERISTICS

In addition to the harmonic characteristics of the blues, certain melodic characteristics may also be found although these are not as essential as the harmonic elements just outlined. In the early days of the great blues singers such as Ma Rainey and Bessie Smith, very often the instrumentalists would try to capture the sound of these singers by flatting certain notes in the same manner as the singers. These flattened notes were the 3rd, 5th, and 7th notes of the major scale. They were called the "blue" notes.

Blue notes in the key of C

Eventually these blue notes evolved into the "blues scale". The blues scale is a scale which may be played over the entire 12 bar blues progression and will sound very effective.

The blues scale is shown below in every key. Only one octave is given, the student should play each scale as written and also an octave higher or lower where-ever possible.

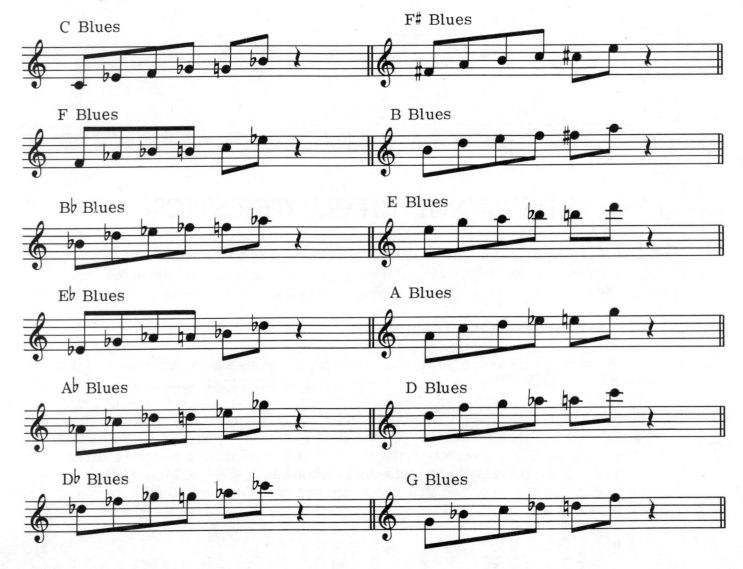

10

BLUES RIFFS

Some of the earliest examples of improvisations based on blues changes produced what came to be known as "riff tunes". A riff is a simple two or four measure melodic phrase usually derived from the blues scale or the notes of the chords or combinations of the two. These "riff tunes" were often improvised spontaneously at jam sessions and very often when musicians were going to jam on the blues they would start by first playing one of these riff tunes and then go on to improvise solos on the changes. The last chorus would be a return to the original riff. Some examples of riff tunes which have become standards are NOW'S THE TIME by Charlie Parker BUD'S BLUES by Bud Powell and JUMPIN' WITH SYMPHONY SID by George Shearing. During the swing era of the 1930s many bands were known as blues bands because almost their whole repetoire consisted of tunes based on the blues. The band of Count Basie was one of the best of the early blues bands.

RIFF TUNES

Below are several examples of riff tunes.

Example I. A combination of blues scale and chord tones. It is a two measure riff. Notice that the V chord in the ninth measure progresses to the I chord in the eleventh measure by going through the IV chord.

Example 2. A four measure riff based on the C blues scale. Notice the V-IV to I in the ninth, tenth and eleventh measures. Note also the break in the riff in the ninth and tenth measure with a return to the original riff in the eleventh measure.

Example 3. A two measure riff repeated on a different note in order to fit the chord change. Notice the use of the II chord in the ninth measure used to prepare the V chord. The II-V progression is again used in the twelfth measure as a device called a TURNAROUND. This is used when going back to the first measure for another chorus. On the last chorus the I chord is used to end the progression.

Example 4. Another four measure riff typical of the kind of tunes played in the bebop era of the 1940s. Notice the alteration of the F♯ to F♮ in measures five and six. This is done to better fit the chords. Again the II-V progression is used in measures nine and ten.

BLUES PATTERNS

In the preface on page 3 I mentioned that every jazz musician has his own collection or repetoire of motives, or licks or patterns that he can draw upon at any moment to fit any chord progression that he may come across. Now we will see how patterns may be used to create a solo. On page 10 you learned the blues scale in every key. Obviously a solo does not consist of just playing up and down a scale. A scale is simply a source from which you can choose the notes that will form your melodic ideas. In other words the scale informs you of the notes which are available on which to create your solo. Below are a number of melodic ideas or patterns created just from the notes of the C blues scale. Try playing each pattern in all the other blues scales. The number of melodic ideas which can be formed from just using the notes of the blues scale are limitless when you consider the number of combinations of notes plus the rhythmic possibilities. Try making up your own patterns, first begin with two measures as shown below then expand your patterns to four measures.

BLUES SOLO

The following solo is based on the blues and is completely madeup from the various patterns given on page 13. Notice that the solo is two choruses long and the turnaround progression is placed in the twelfth measure of the first chorus. Remember that if you are being accompanied by a chordal instrument such as piano or guitar the necessary transposition must be kept in mind.

While the above solo may be an exggerated use of the idea of memorized patterns it does illustrate the value and the need for building a repetoire of good patterns which can be played over the more commonly used chord progressions. We will now go on to see how to go about making up your own patterns.

APPROACHES TO IMPROVISATION

There are four basic approaches to improvising on a particular set of chord changes.

VERTICALLY or CHORDALLY- This approach is used particulary where there are many chords in the progression usually occuring every two counts. In this situation the player may want to base his solo mostly on the notes of the chord. A good example of that kind of playing is shown in the recordings of tenor saxophonist Coleman Hawkins. John Coltrane's recording of GIANT STEPS is an example of chordal playing. Great care must be taken that the solo doesn't just sound like an exercise in arpeggios.

HORIZONTAL or SCALAR- This approach is used where the composition contains few chords and therefore the player in order to generate interest must use all the availble notes at his disposal. He would use all of the notes of the scale from which the chords are derived. For example for a C7 chord he would use the entire F scale. There are also a number of scale choices other than the original scale which may be used to create interest. The example of the solo based on the blues scale (page 14) is an example of that type of playing even though there are more chord tones than scale tones. The idea is that you are playing and thinking in terms of a scale rather than a chord. Tenor saxophonist Lester Young was a horizontal player.

COMBINATION OF THE ABOVE- Most good jazz players obviously use some combination of the chordal and scale approaches in their improvisations. An analysis of the solos by alto saxophonist Charlie Parker will show a good balance between chordal playing and scalar playing. An analysis of a good number of Parker's solos will also show his fondness for using a number of patterns over and over again throughout his solos.

MOTIVIC- This approach to improvisation is based on motifs, short melodic phrases which the improvisor attempts to develop through various devices such as inverting the intervals of the motive, sequential repetition, rhythmic alteration, and melodic alteration. A classic example of this type of playing is the recording by tenor saxophonist Sonny Rollins on a tune called BLUE 7.

Each of the above approaches to improvisation will be explored throughout this book.

PLAYING THROUGH THE CHANGES

One of the first requirements of any jazz performer is to be able to play through the "changes" (chords) of any given tune or progression. The following series of studies, which are based on the blues progression, are designed to show the student how to develop that ability.

MODERN BLUES PROGRESSION

Before beginning our studies it is important that you understand the differences between the blues progression you will be working from in this section of the book and the blues progression shown in the first section of the book starting on page 9. There are many variations of blues progressions and the progressions you have just played through are the most basic of all. However, in order to increase the melodic possibilities we will have to now use a progression which contains more chords. You will notice that the chord shown in measure 1 is now a major 7th chord. Notice also the II chord in measure 3, This Chord is used to prepare the G7 in measure 4. (See page 8) The chords in measures 11 and 12 are called "turnaround" chords and prepare you to repeat the progression by taking you back to the 1st measure.

BLUES PROGRESSION IN HALF NOTES

This first study shows an example of playing through the blues by using just half notes. By using half notes it allows you time to think better. Notice how melodic lines are created by moving from one chord to the next chord either a half step or a whole step away. See meas, 1 to meas. 2, meas. 5 to meas. 6, to meas. 7 to meas. 8 to meas. 9 to meas. 10.

BLUES PROGRESSION IN QUARTER NOTES

This next study requires that you think a little faster because the melodic line is based on quarter notes. Notice the smooth movement from meas. 1 to meas. 2, again from meas. 3 to meas. 4. to meas. 5,6,7,8,9,10. The line picks up again from meas.11 to meas. 12.

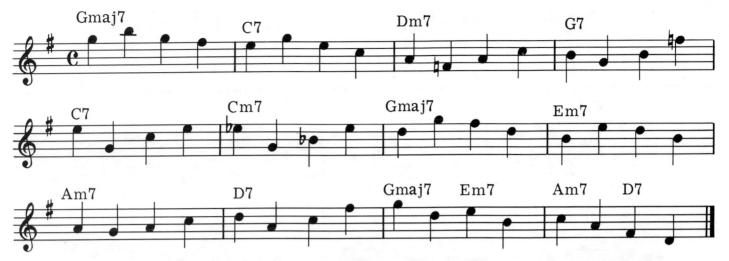

BLUES PROGRESSION IN EIGHTH NOTES

The following study is based on playing through the blues progression using eighth notes. Notice the smooth movement from chord to chord in meas. 1 through meas. 9. and again from meas. 11 to meas. 12.

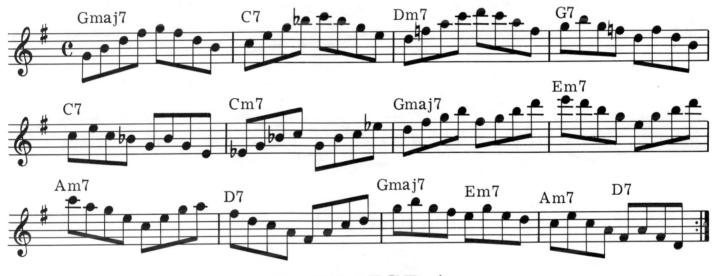

EXERCISE 1.

Below is the blues progression in the key of C. The student should play through the changes in the same manner as the previous three studies. Remember to create your own patterns. You may change the direction of the melodic line at any point in the chord.

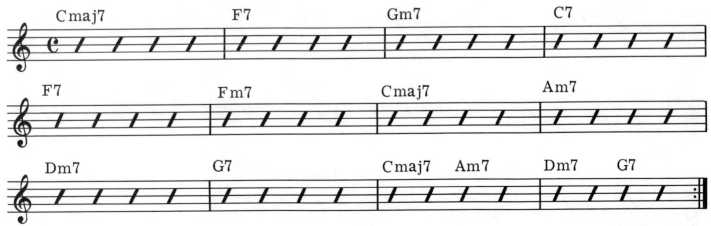

BLUES PROGRESSION IN TRIPETS

The following study is based on the blues progression played in triplets.

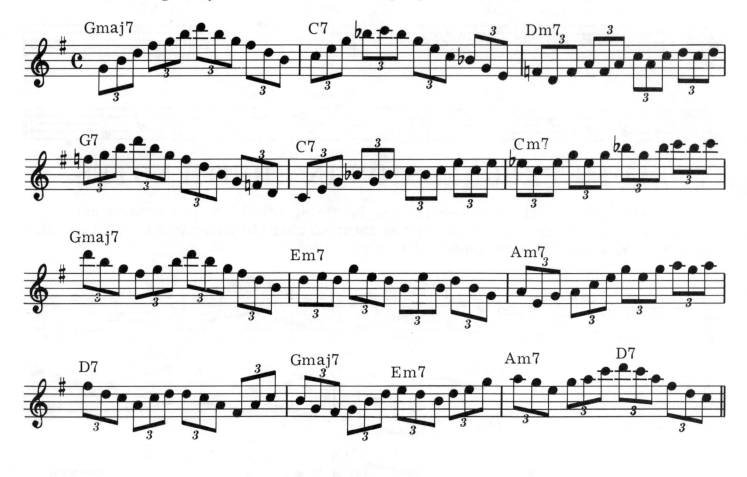

EXERCISE 2.

Below is the same progression in the key of D. The student should play through the changes in triplets as above, REMEMBER that you can change the direction of your line at any point. You may also go from any chord tone to any other chord tone. It is not necessary to go in consecutive order.

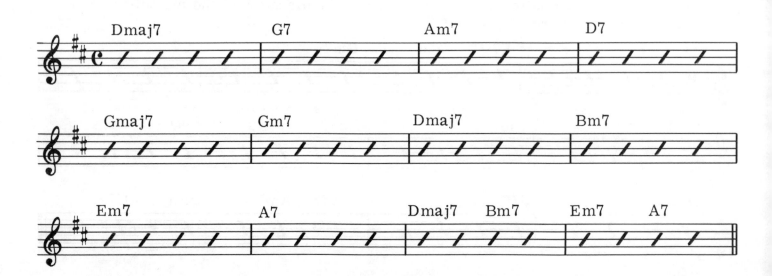

BLUES PROGRESSION IN SIXTEENTH NOTES

This next study is based on the blues progression played in sixteenth notes.

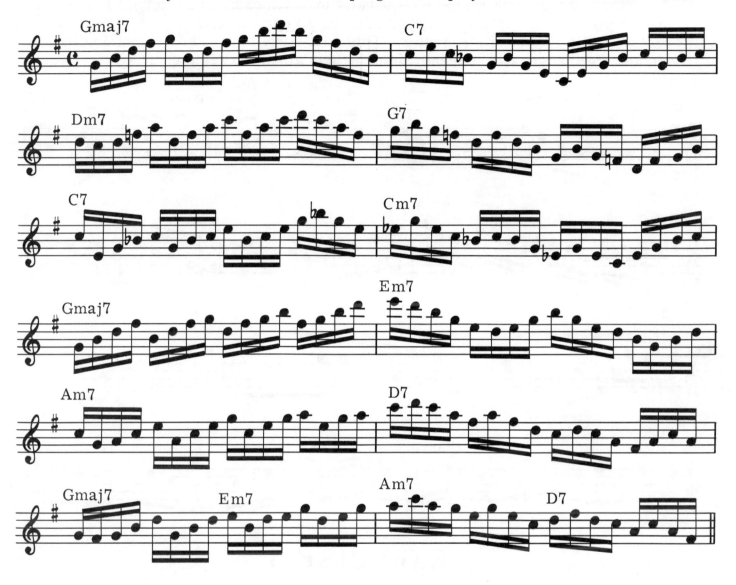

EXERCISE 3.

Play through the following blues progression in the key of F using sixteenth notes.

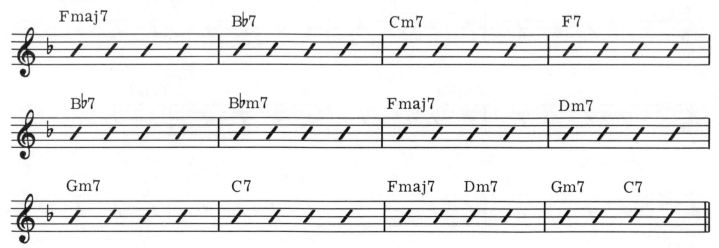

COMBINING RHYTHMS

Since interest in a jazz solo is usually maintained by introducing various and unexpected rhythms, the jazz player must be able to move from one rhythm to another while keeping a steady beat. This next study is based on combining the eighth note, triplet and sixteenth note rhythms all in the same chorus.

EXERCISE 4.

This next blues progression is in the key of A. Play through the changes by using combinations of the rhythms you just learned.

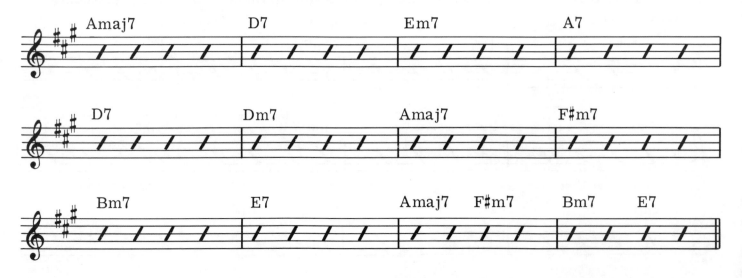

RHYTHM PATTERNS
RESTS

A good jazz solo should not be just a very long series of uninterrupted notes. Just as a good speaker knows how to leave places to breathe in order to make his speech more effective, a jazz player must also know where to leave breath-thing space in his melodies. This allows the audiance a chance to catch his breath as he subconsciously trys to follow the flow of the melodic line. These breathing places which we call rests in music, also gives the melodic line its shape and musical expression. A good test is to try singing your solo before playing and take note of where you would normally breath. The same breathing places should take place in your melodic line.

Below are a number of examples of rhythm patterns containing breathing places or rests. Play through each example.

The following example of the blues shows the application of the rests shown above. Every two measures uses one of the above examples.

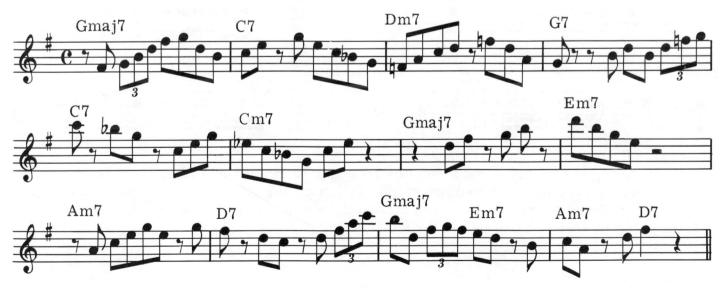

EXERCISE 5.

Here is a blues progression in the key of Bb . play through the chords using the rhythm patterns shown on page 21.

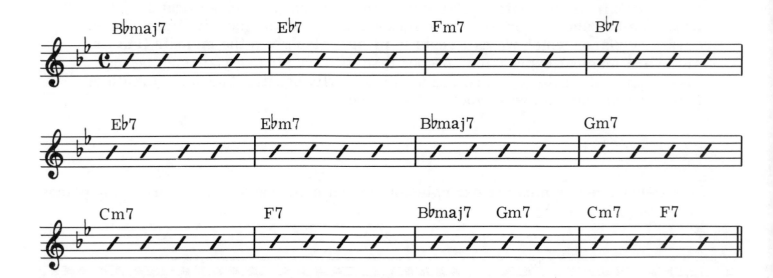

MORE RHYTHM PATTERNS

When improvising at a slower tempo it's possible to play more notes to each beat. The following examples are based on combinations of sixteenth notes and rests.

Note; At this point you should be listening to recordings of various jazz players and trying to write down some rhythm patterns that you like. After awhile these patterns shaped to your own taste will become a part of your own repetoire of patterns that you can use in your own soloing.

Here again is the blues progression using the rhythm patterns given on page 22. Remember that the tempo is SLOW.

EXERCISE 5.

Here is the blues in E♭ play through the changes using the rhythm patterns given on page 22.

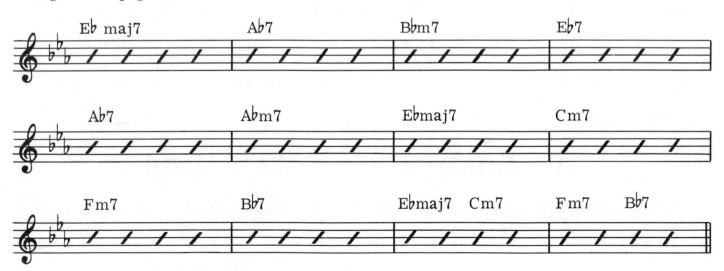

SCALAR (HORIZONTAL) APPROACH TO IMPROVISATION

So far all our examples of improvisations have been based purely on chord tones which has limited our melodic possibilties and produced almost exercise-like sounding solos. Now we will study the scalar or horizontal approach to improvisation.

MODES-IMPROVISING SCALES

Earlier in the book (page 6), you learned that all chords are derived from scales. In the scalar approach to improvisation we will base our improvisations on the scales from which the chords of the progression are derived.

MAJOR SCALE(IONIAN MODE)

Referring back to page 6 you learned that the major 7th chord is formed from the 1st, 3rd, 5th and 7th notes of the major scale (the ionian mode) Another major 7th chord is formed from the lydian mode however in almost all cases the major 7th chord used is the I chord.

II CHORD-DORIAN MODE

The II chord built on the 2nd step of the major scale uses the dorian mode as its improvising scale. Although there are also minor 7th chords built on the 3rd step (III chord) and 6th step (VI chord) in the majority of situations the minor 7th will be considered a primary chord as in the II-V-I progression and will use the dorian mode as its improvising scale.

V CHORD-MIXOLYDIAN MODE

Since there is only one dominant 7th chord (V chord) in any key. The mixolydian mode will be used as its improvising scale. Later in the course you will learn of other scales which may also be used for improvising on the V chord.

DORIAN (SCALES) MODES

Before attempting to improvise on the scales it is important that you first know the scales. Below are all the Dorian modes. Play each mode an octave higher or lower wherever possible. You should always use the full range of your instrument.

MIXOLYDIAN MODES

Below are all the mixolydian modes. The chord symbol which is related to the mode is also indicated. Play each mode an octave higher or lower wherever possible.

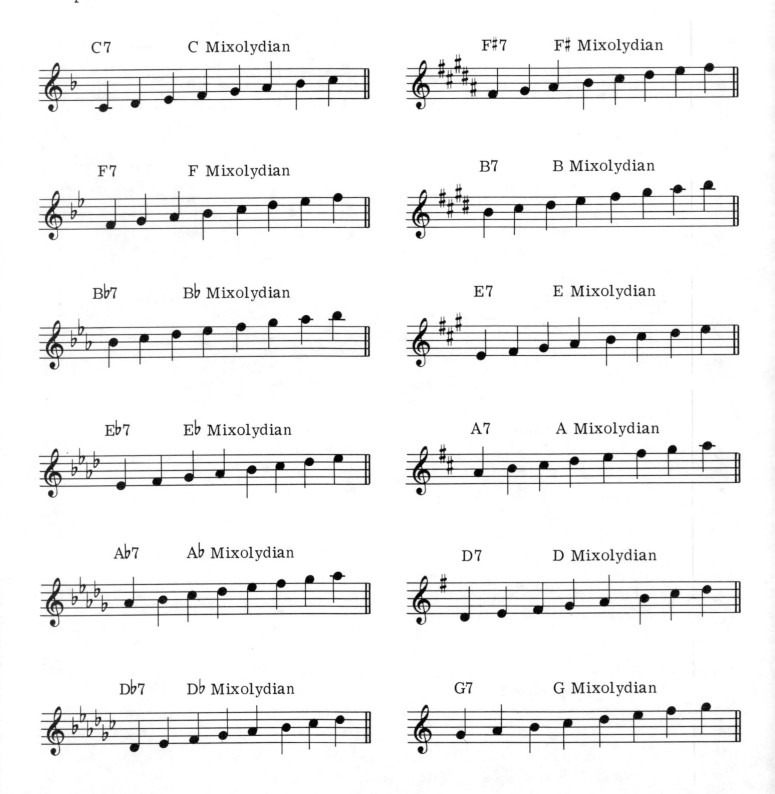

BLUES PROGRESSION WITH SUBSTITUTE CHORDS

There are many variations on the basic blues progression, below is just one more example of the progression used by the more advanced jazz players. The reasons for the new chords are outlined as follows.

Measure 6. In all our previous examples we used a Minor 7th chord in this measure, Now we treat the minor 7th as a II chord and follow that with its V chord (F7).

Measure. 7. In jazz harmony the III chord is often used as a substitute chord for the I chord, therefore Bm7 is used as a substitute for the GMaj7.

Measure 8. The VI chord which we have used up till now is normally a minor chord, but we will now alter it to a dominant 7th chord in order to create a II - V situation in measures 7 and 8.

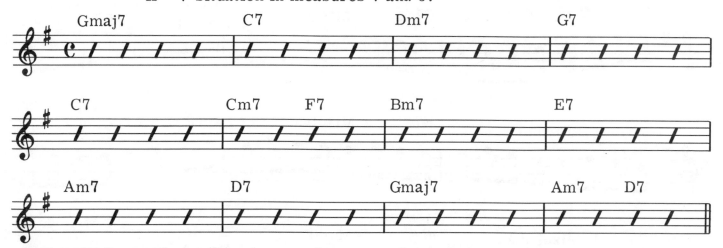

BLUES PROGRESSION WITH RELATED SCALES

Our next series of improvisations will be based on scale tones rather than chords which we have been using up till now. Below is the blues progression shown above with the scales or modes for each chord also indicated.

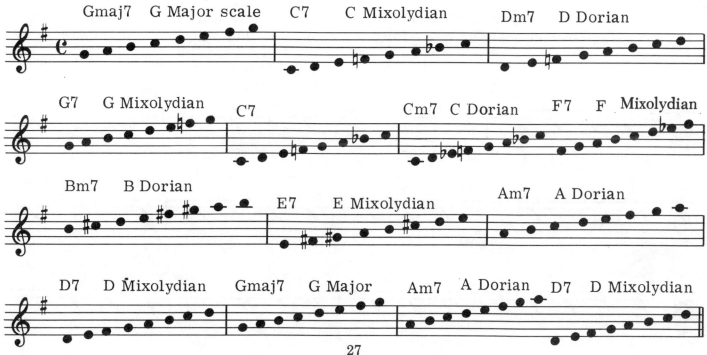

IMPROVISING ON SCALES
USING EIGHTH NOTES

Below is an example of a possible improvisation based on the blues progression shown on page 27. The improvisation is based on the scales or modes from which each of the chords are derived. At this point you should be familliar with the dorian modes shown on page 25 and the mixolydian modes shown on page 26.

EXERCISE 6.

Here is the same progression in the key of C. Play through the progression using the correct scale or mode for each chord. At this point use only eighth notes.

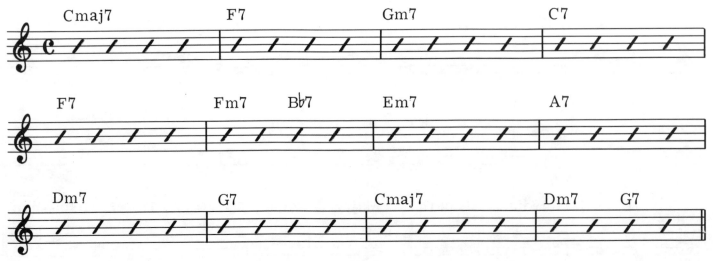

SCALE TONES IN TRIPLETS

The following improvisation is based on **scale** tones played in triplets. The scale or mode being used is **also** indicated.

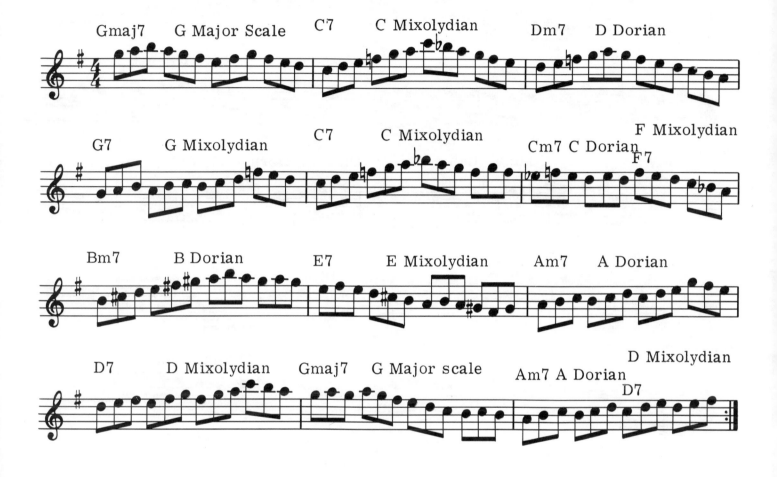

EXERCISE 7.

Here is the blues progression in the key of A. Use the triplet rhythm and create an improvisation based on the scale or modal tones.

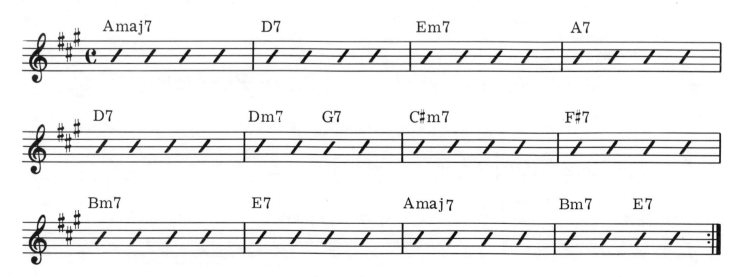

SCALE TONES IN SIXTEENTH NOTES

This next improvisation is based on scale tones played as sixteenth notes.

EXERCISE 8.

The following progression is in the key of F. Create an improvisation using only scale or modal tones and based on sixteenth notes.

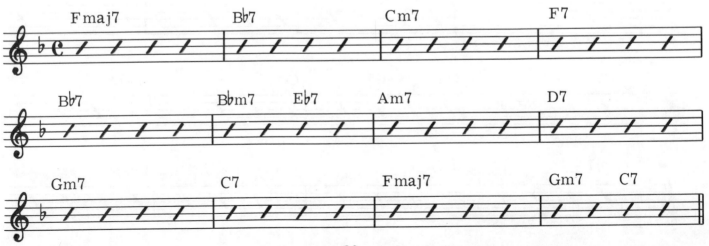

COMBINING RHYTHMS AND SCALE TONES

This next improvisation combines eighth notes, triplets and sixteenth notes. All the notes are derived from the scales or modes as indicated by the chord symbols.

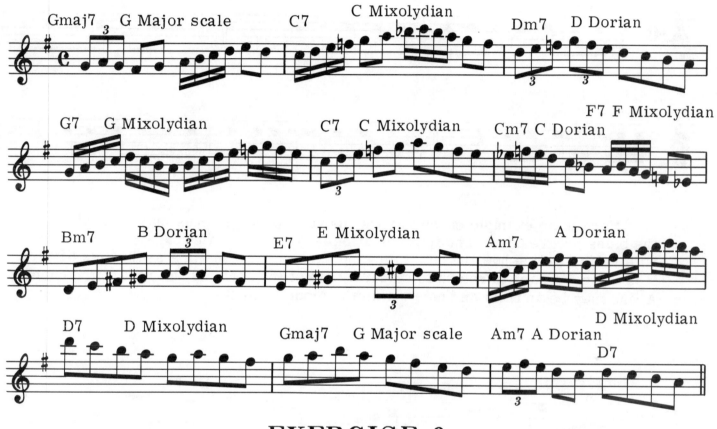

EXERCISE 9.

The following progression is in the key of A. Create an improvisation based on scale or modal tones using combinations of eighth notes, triplets and sixteenth notes as shown above. Be sure to use the correct mode for each chord.

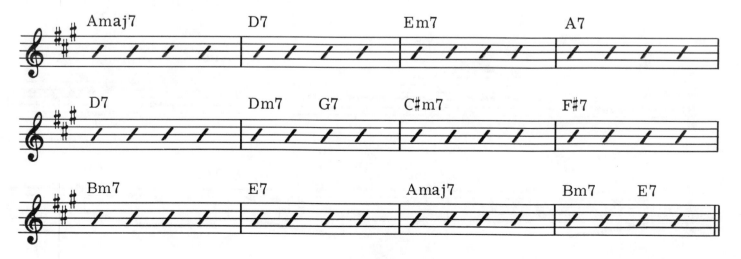

COMBINED SCALE TONES AND RESTS

Just as we used rests in combination with chord tones earlier in our lessons, now we'll use rests with scale tones. Below is a series of six different rhythm patterns which show rests occuring on different beats in each measure.

Here is an example of the way the above rhythm patterns may be applied to the blues progression. The improvisation is based on scale tones in combination with rests. Notice how the note following each rest moves in a scale wise pattern. It is not necessary to return to the first note of the scale or the root of the chord. A line may begin from any note within the mode or scale.

EXERCISE 10.

Here is the blues progression in the key of B♭. Create an improvisation based on scale tones using the rhythm patterns shown on page 32.

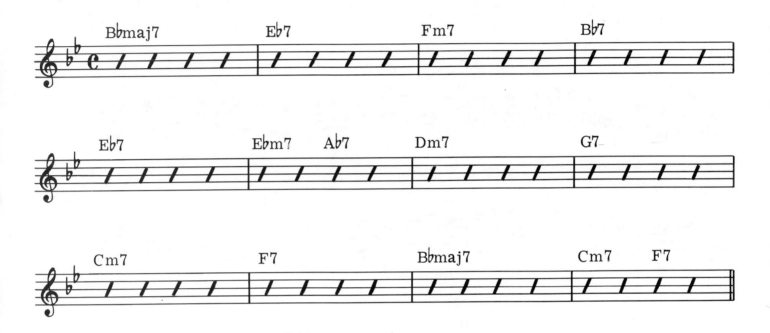

RESTS AND SIXTEENTH NOTE PATTERNS

The following rhythm patterns are based on combinations of sixteenth notes, eighth notes and rests.

Here is an improvisation using the rhythm patterns shown on page 33. Each pattern is used twice through the twelve measures. Remember that the tempo is slow.

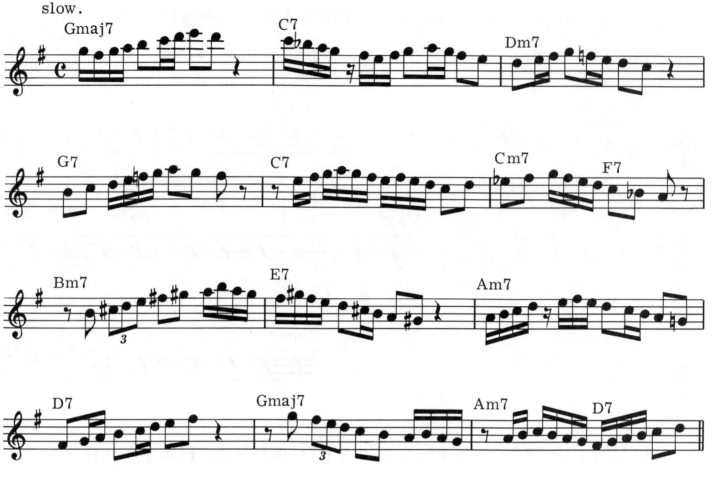

EXERCISE 11.

Here is the blues in the key of E♭. Create an improvisation using the rhythm patterns given on page 33. Remember to use only scale tones.

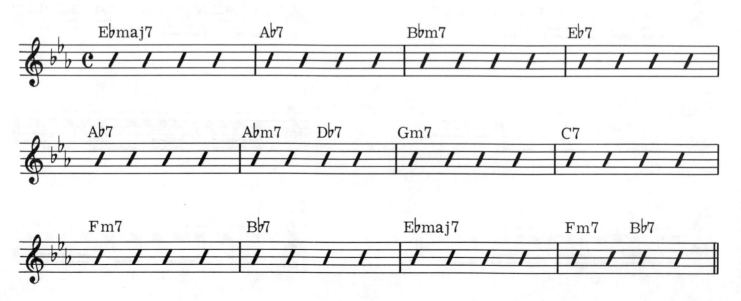

COMBINING CHORD TONES AND SCALE TONES

Although some jazz performers develop one approach more extensively than others, some preferring to play more scalar while others prefer to play more chordally, the most interesting players seem to develop an approach which incorporates both scalar and chordal playing. The distinguishing aspects of one player from another is in the choice of notes, the balance between scale and chord tones, the sound that each player gets on their particular instrument, the use of certain rhythm patterns, the overall rhythmic feeling, and included in the improvisation the use of blues notes. Below is an example which combines scale and chord tones and includes also the free use of blues notes. The rhythm patterns are not restricted but do include some of the patterns used in earlier lessons.

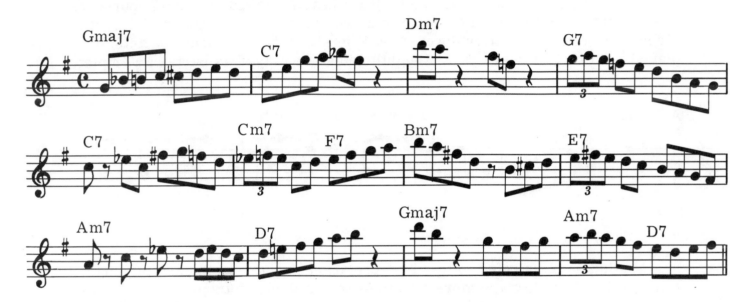

Here is another example of combining scale tones and chord tones. This should be played at a slower tempo than the example given above.

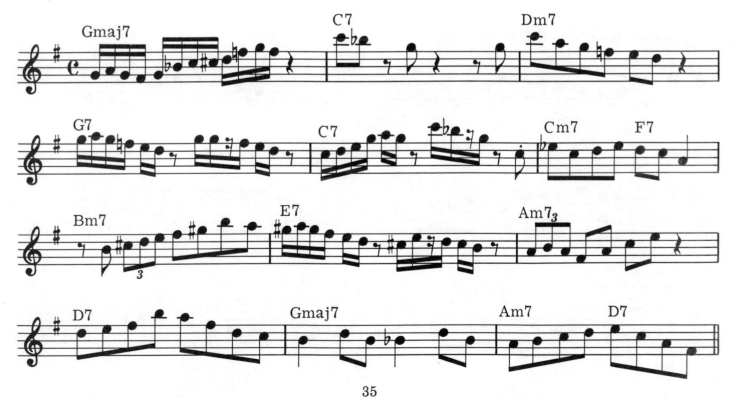

MODERN RHYTHMIC CONCEPT

One of the important elements in any jazz performance is the "jazz feel". or "swing feel". that the artist brings to his music. This jazz or swing feeling is best described as a kind of loose feeling applied to a series of eighth notes as opposed to the very exact, rigid feeling given to the same series of eighth notes when played by a marching band or a rock band.

EIGHTH NOTES IN THE JAZZ STYLE

This jazz feel is best understood if we hear it played or for our purposes see it notated. Below is an example of a two measure jazz pattern. First it is given as it would be written down, then it is shown how it should be actually played. Notice that every pair of eighth notes are played as parts of a triplet.

As written   As played

Musicians often refer to this interpretation of eighth notes as "playing with a triplet feel". Below are more examples of the triplet interpretation of playing eighth notes.

EXTENDING THE CHORDS

Up to this point we have studied several approaches to creating a jazz solo. First we improvised on the notes of the three basic 7th chords, the major 7th, the dominant 7th and the minor 7th. This is called chordal or vertical playing. Secondly we improvised on the notes contained in the chord related scales, the major scale for the major 7th chord, the mixolydian mode for the dominant 7th chord and the dorian mode for the minor 7th chord. This is the scalar or horizontal approach. And then we combined both techniques which is how most good jazz performers improvise. Now for a while let's go back to the chordal approach to creating a solo and explore the melodic possibilities when we extend the chords beyond the 7th. Below is a listing of the possible extensions of the major 7th chord. Notice the major 6th chord, although not an extension of the major 7th it is a very commonly used chord in place of, or along with, the major 7th. Notice also that the 6th and the 13th are the same letter name. The formula indicates the scale position of each chord note and is based on the major scale.

CHORD	FORMULA	SYMBOL	CHORD	FORMULA	SYMBOL
Major 6th	1,3,5,6	6	Major 6/9	1,3,5,6,9	6/9
Major 7th	1,3,5,7	Maj7	Major 9#11	1,3,5,7,9,#11	Maj9#11
Major 7/6	1,3,5,6,7	Maj7/6	Major 13th	1,3,5,7,9,13	Maj13
Major 9th	1,3,5,7,9	Maj9	Major 13#11	1,3,5,7,9,#11,13	Maj13#11

Notice that when the 11th is used with a major chord it is generally a raised or augmented 11th. The raised 11th is the same as the raised 4th.

MAJOR CHORD RUNS

A very important part of every jazz student's studies is the collecting and the memorization, of a number of runs or licks or patterns that he can instantly draw upon to play against the more commonly used chords or series of chords. The following runs are all based on the G major chord and should be memorized and then played in all keys. Notice that as you extend the chord up to the 9th, 11th and 13th, you may wonder why it is necessary to learn these extended chords since all of these notes are contained in the major scale. The answer is that you could use the major scale just as we did in the previous studies, however, by learning to use these extended chords it helps to avoid the over use of scale-like or exercise sounding solos and helps to encourage a better melodic concept.

38

EXTENDED DOMINANT 7th CHORDS

The dominant 7th chord is derived from the mixolydian mode (see page 26). This chord also may be extended and below we see the formula for extending the dominant 7th chord. The formula is based on the mixolydian mode so that 1,3,5,7,9 means that those notes, the 1st, 3rd, 5th, 7th, and 9th notes come out of the mixolydian mode. Remember that the mixolydian mode is also referred to as the dominant 7th scale.

CHORD	FORMULA	SYMBOL	CHORD	FORMULA	SYMBOL
Dominant 7th	1,3,5,7	7	Dominant 7/6	1,3,5,6,7	7/6
Dominant 9th	1,3,5,7,9	9	Dominant 13th	1,3,5,7,9,13	13

DOMINANT 7th CHORD RUNS

Below are a whole batch of runs based on the dominant 7th type chords. These runs should be memorized and transposed to all keys so that you have a good repetoire of runs that you can play against any dominant 7th type chord. After a while you should be able to create your own runs to add to your collection.

DOMINANT 7th CHORD SCALE RUNS

The following runs combine the extended chord tones and scale tones: The difference between the following runs and what is shown on page 39 is that you can now enlarge your melodic concept and not be limited to using scale tones as simply notes used to connect two chord tones. All runs are based on the D7 chord.

EXTENDED MINOR 7th CHORDS

The minor 7th chord that we are interested in at this time is the chord derived from the dorian mode (see page 25). This chord is also referred to as the II chord as shown on page 7. The chord may be extended and below we see the formula for the various extensions. Remember that the formula refers to the notes of the dorian mode and the scale is sometimes referred to as the minor 7th scale.

CHORD	FORMULA	SYMBOL
Minor 7th	1, 3, 5, 7	m7
Minor 9th	1, 3, 5, 7, 9	m9
Minor 11th	1, 3, 5, 7, 9, 11	m11

MINOR 7th CHORD RUNS

The following runs are based on the minor type runs listed above. Memorize any runs that you prefer and transpose them to all the other keys.

41

MELODIC EMBELLISHMENT

Up to now, virtually our entire focus has been on developing jazz solos through using chord tones and scale tones. However there are other notes which may be used to help create a smoother melodic line and to increase the musical interest of any melodic line, these other notes are called CHROMATIC TONES. Chromatic tones are those notes which are not part of any scale.

Below we see the chromatic tones in each of the three kinds of scales we learned so far. The scale tones are shown as whole notes and the chromatic tones are the smaller black notes. Remember that each sharped note may also be called by its enharmonic equivalent. Ex. C# = Db.

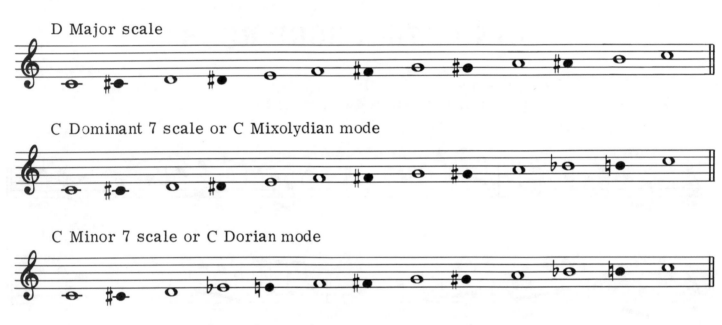

D Major scale

C Dominant 7 scale or C Mixolydian mode

C Minor 7 scale or C Dorian mode

LOWER NEIGHBOR TONES

Every scale or chord tone has a note a half step below it which is known as its LOWER NEIGHBOR TONE. These neighboring tones are usually chromatic tones but occasionaly a lower neighbor may also be another scale tone. See below.

C Scale with lower neighbors; LN

LN   LN   LN   LN   LN   LN   LN   LN

Notice that the 3rd and 7th tones of the scale are lower neighbor tones since they are a half step below their next scale tone.

LOWER NEIGHBOR STUDIES

The following studies are based on using the lower neighbor tones through a variety of chord types.

43

UPPER NEIGHBOR TONES

Besides having a lower neighbor, each chord tone and scale tone has two kinds of upper neighbors. 1) An upper neighbor may be a note which is a half-step above a given note. 2) Another kind of upper neighbor may be a note which is one scale-step above the given note.

SCALE STEP UPPER NEIGHBOR

The following examples show the use of the scale step upper neighbor tones.

FMaj9

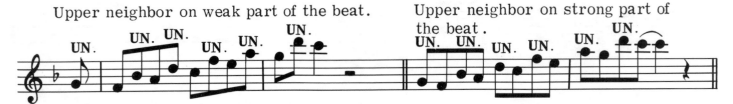

Notice in the first measure the upper neighbor is played on the beat and then it appears on the "and" of the 3rd beat. In the second measure there is a lower neighbor on the "and" of the 3rd beat.

FMaj9

The following example uses upper neighbors on weak and strong beats.

FMaj9

The following examples show different ways of rephrasing the same melody.

44

HALF STEP UPPER NEIGHBOR

The half step upper neighbor is not as popular among jazz players as the scale step upper neighbor. Below is an example of its use.

A more common use of the half step upper neighbor is shown below. It is used as a passing tone between two adjacent scale tones or a scale tone and a chord tone. All examples are based on the C7th scale.

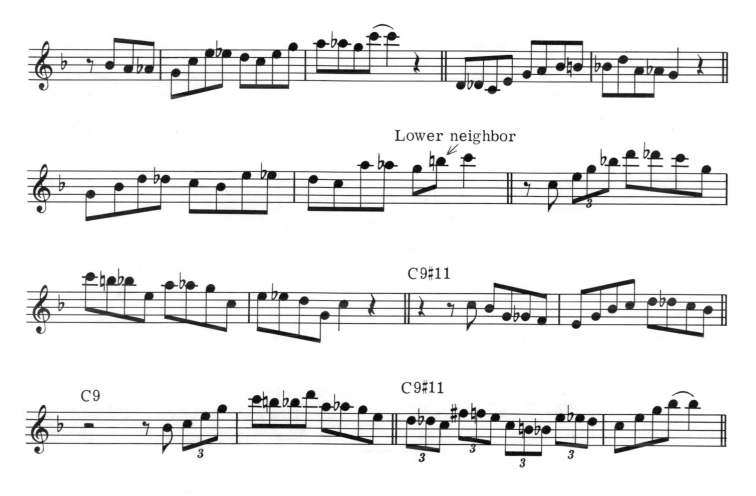

The chromatic passing tone may actually be thought of as either a lower or upper neighbor tone.

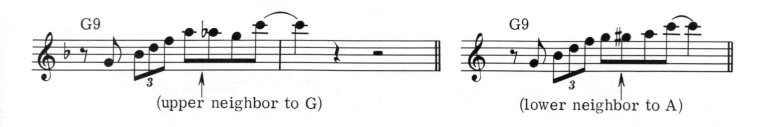

(upper neighbor to G)   (lower neighbor to A)

COMBINING UPPER AND LOWER NEIGHBOR TONES.

Any note may be embellished in a number of different ways by using combinations of upper and lower neighboring tones. Below are several example of embellishing the notes of a pure C major chord.

Upper and lower neighbors embellishing each note of the C major scale.

Here are a variety of chords using lower and upper neighbors.

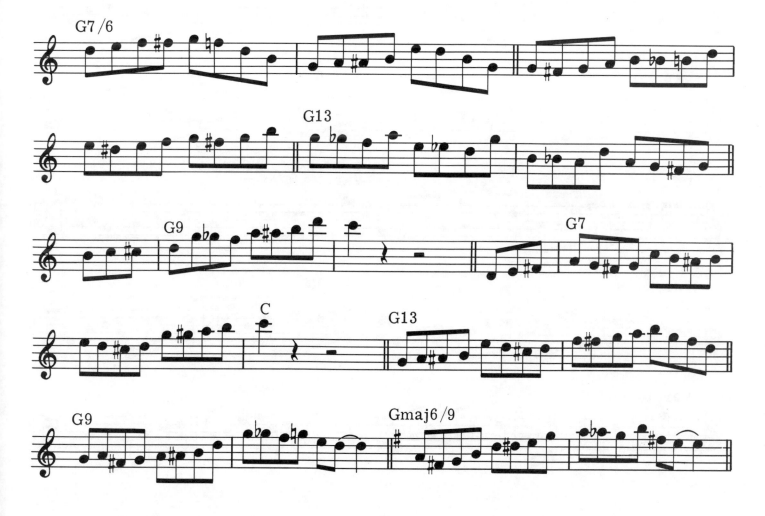

MELODIC DEVELOPMENT

To create interesting melodies requires more than a knowledge of chords and scales and theoretical expertise. Listening to recordings by the jazz greats has been the most important teaching aid for any musician who wants to become a jazz player. However there are a number of techniques or devices that one can learn which will help in learning how to develop more interesting melodies. One of the ways in which melodies can be made more interesting is through the most essential element in jazz; rhythmic interest. The continued use of eighth notes over a long period of time can become boring and so it is important to be able to take any melodic phrase and know how to play it in a variety of rhythmical patterns. Below is an example of a melodic phrase played in all eighth notes and then the same phrase played in a number of other rhythms.

REPETITION

Repetition is one of the most basic ways of developing an idea. The repetition of a melodic phrase creates tension which is released when a new melodic phrase is introduced. This principle of "tension and release" is of prime importance in creating a good jazz solo. In all the three elements of music, melody, rhythm and harmony there is tension and release. In analysing any number of good jazz solos one can see a good balance of patterns of tension and release.

The following examples illustrate the various ways of using repetition. All examples are based on the first four bars of the blues progression.

Example 1 shows a short melodic phrase which is repeated twice with the last phrase slightly extended as a sort of release to the tension setup by the repetition of the phrase.

Example 2 shows the same melodic phrase but occuring on different beats of the measure.

Example 3 shows the same phrase but rhythmic variation.

Example 4 shows the rhythmic repetition but the melody varies.

Example 5 shows the same melodic phrase with pickup notes.

It should be understood that a prolonged use of repetition can lead to a loss of interest on the part of the listener. Too much predictability leads to boredom. Of course this does depend on the melody which is being used and the length of the melody. A melodic phrase which occupies one measure cannot be repeated too often. A melody that occupys two measures allows the listener more time to absorb what he's heard before the repetition starts in again and so boredom does not set in as quickly. Review the section on riffs which begins on page 11. The riff is another example of a repeated melodic phrase.

SEQUENCE

Another form of repetition is the "sequence". A sequence is a repetition of a melodic phrase with each repetition beginning on a different pitch. Some sequential phrases are played either a step higher or lower or at a predetermined symmetrical interval. The following examples will illustrate the various types of sequential patterns.

Example 1. Sequence based on notes within the same chord. Notice that the first notes of each repetition forms a descending melodic line.

Example 1a. Another sequence based on the same Gmaj9th chord but the first note of each repetition now forms an ascending melodic line.

Example 2. sequence based on a very common progression. Notice again that each repetition begins on a note within the chord and forms an ascending melodic line.

Example 2a same progression as above with repetition starting on different note within the chord.

50

Example 2b same progression but notice how the notes in each repetition are adjusted to fit the chords.

Example 3. Sequence ascending in thirds based on chord progression above.

Example 4. Sequence occupies two counts.   Example 5. Sequence occupies two counts.

Example 6. Sequence occupies two counts.   Example 7. Sequence occupies one meas.

MORE BLUES

The following blues choruses illustrate the various melodic embellishments outlined on the previous pages. Note the use of repetition in the 1st and 2nd measures. There is a slight adjustment to fit the chord in the 2nd measure. Note the use of sequences in measures 4, 6, 9 and 10. Notice also the use of upper and lower neighboring tones.

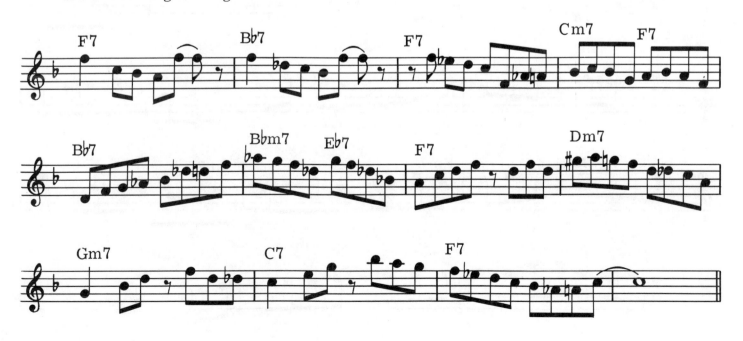

The following blues solo begins with a repetitive melodic phrase in measures 1, 2 and 3. A sequence occurs in measures 7, 8 and 9. Another sequence occurs in measures 9 and 10. Notice also the use of lower and upper neighbor tones particularly as approach tones to measures 6, 7, 9, 10. 11 and 12.

This next blues solo begins with a sequence in measures 1 and 2. Notice also the extensive use of upper and lower neighbor tones to create a smooth flow to the melodic line.

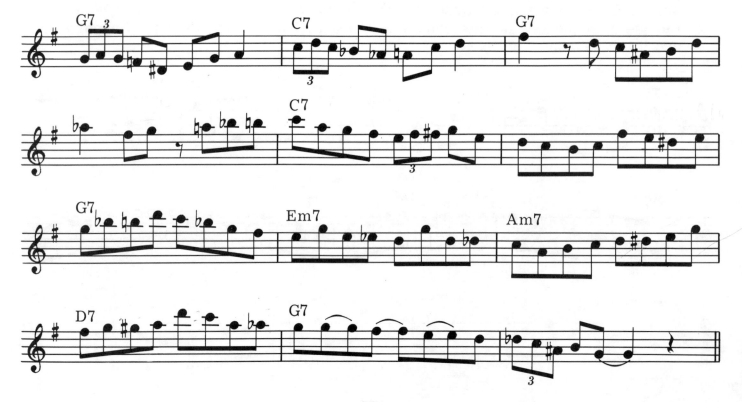

This next blues opens with a repetition of the melodic phrase in measures 1 and 2 There is a slight change in measure 4 but the rhythmic pattern remains the same as in measure 2. Note the extensive use of upper and lower neighbor tones. Rhythmic interest is caused by an interesting use of rhythmic patterns. The blues scale is used in measures 11 and 12.

For a complete contrast to the solo above, the following blues solo is much rhythmically simpler. Notice the frequent use of rests. The two note rhythm pattern shown in measure two is repeated throughout the solo. Notice also the use of the blue note (flatted 3rd of B♭) in the 6th measure. This blue note helps to create a melodic line on the first note of the 5th, 6th, and 7th measures.

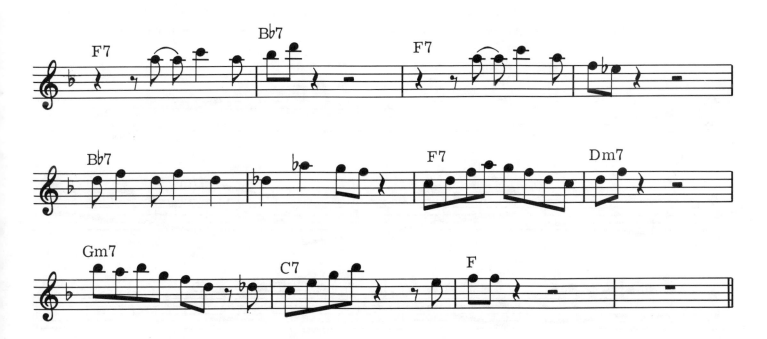

MOTIFS

One of the most inventive and creative ways of developing a solo is to work a MOTIF into your solo. This motif which may be a melodic phrase of as little as two or three notes acts as a unifying element recurring throughout the solo and gives the aware listener an opportunity to identify with your improvisation. It creates a connection between the soloist and the listener.

The following solo is based on a melodic phrase taken from a previous solo. The motif is announced in the first measure and then is repeatedly altered rhythmically. Notice how the motif is spread through two measures starting from the 2nd half of the 4th measure. In the 7th measure it is started and in the 8th measure the motif is played in another key. Another key in the 9th and 10th measures and may still be heard in the 11th measure.

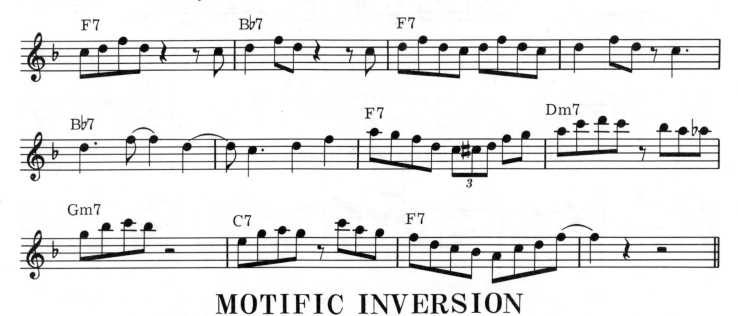

MOTIFIC INVERSION

The direction of an interval within a motif may be changed in order to create variety in your solo. Notice in the following example the motif in measures 1 and 2 are based on the interval of a 4th followed by a 3rd, both intervals in ascending order. Notice that in measure 5 the interval between the third and fourth notes is a 4th but it descends. The same thing occurs in measure 7. Notice too that the motif appears only occasionally throughout the solo otherwise it would lead to boredom.

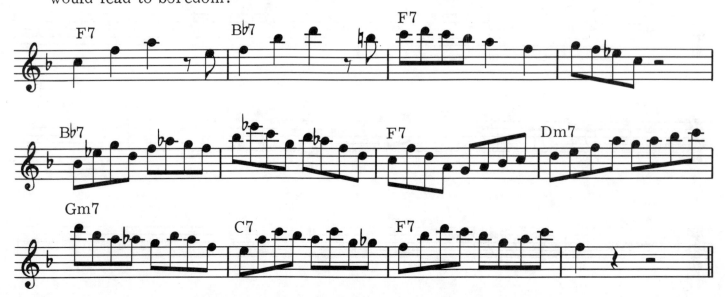

MINOR SCALES-MINOR KEYS

Although jazz has been historically a major scale music, there are some tunes or segments of tunes which are played in the minor mode. In fact in recent years there has been a growing number of tunes written in the minor mode. A brief explanation of minor scales and minor keys follows.

All major scales have a relative minor scale. These relative minor scales start, or have as their tonic note, the 6th note of the major scale. Below are the relative minor scales for C major.

1. The PURE or NATURAL MINOR SCALE. This scale follows the notes of its relative major scale without any alterations.

A Pure or Natural Minor Scale

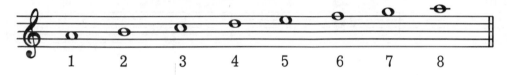

2. The HARMONIC MINOR SCALE. This scale contains a raised (half-step) 7th.

A Harmonic Minor

3. The MELODIC MINOR SCALE. As this scale ascends the 6th and 7th tones are raised a half-step. As the scale descends the 6th and 7th are returned to their normal pitch.

A Melodic Minor

4. The JAZZ MINOR SCALE. Although not used in classical music, this scale is widely used by jazz musicians. Both ascending and descending forms contain the raised 6th and 7th tones.

A Jazz Minor

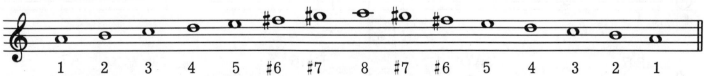

Notice that the major scales and their relative minor scale share the SAME key signature. (that of the major scale). All alterations occur only in the music.

MINOR BLUES

Up until the late 1950's almost all blues were played in major keys, however, from that time on musicians have explored the minor blues with greater frequency. The chords which makeup the minor blues progressions are a derivative of all of the minor scale forms including the dorian mode which contains the important flatted 3rd, the characteristic sound of the minor mode. Since the chords are not derived from one particular scale the tonic or, the I chord, is optional. It might be a minor 6th, a minor-major 7th, a minor 7th or just a pure minor triad. The following minor blues progression is just one of a number of possible progressions. Notice that the I chord is given as a minor 6. Notice also that the chord in the second measure is a V7 ♭9 rather then the usual IV chord as in the major key. The ♭9 is included in all V7 chords since it reenforces the minor sound.

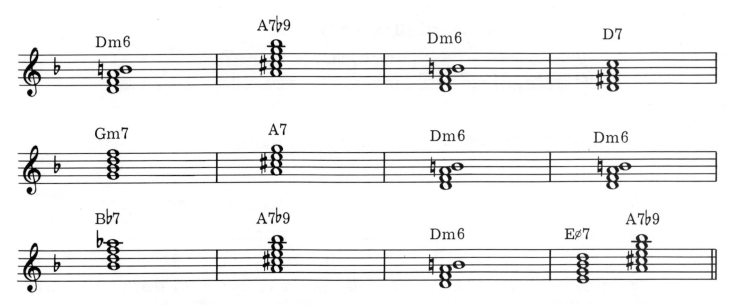

IMPROVISATION BASED ON HALF NOTES

The following example of an improvisation is based on chord tones played in half notes.

56

IMPROVISATION BASED ON CHORD
TONES USING QUARTER NOTES

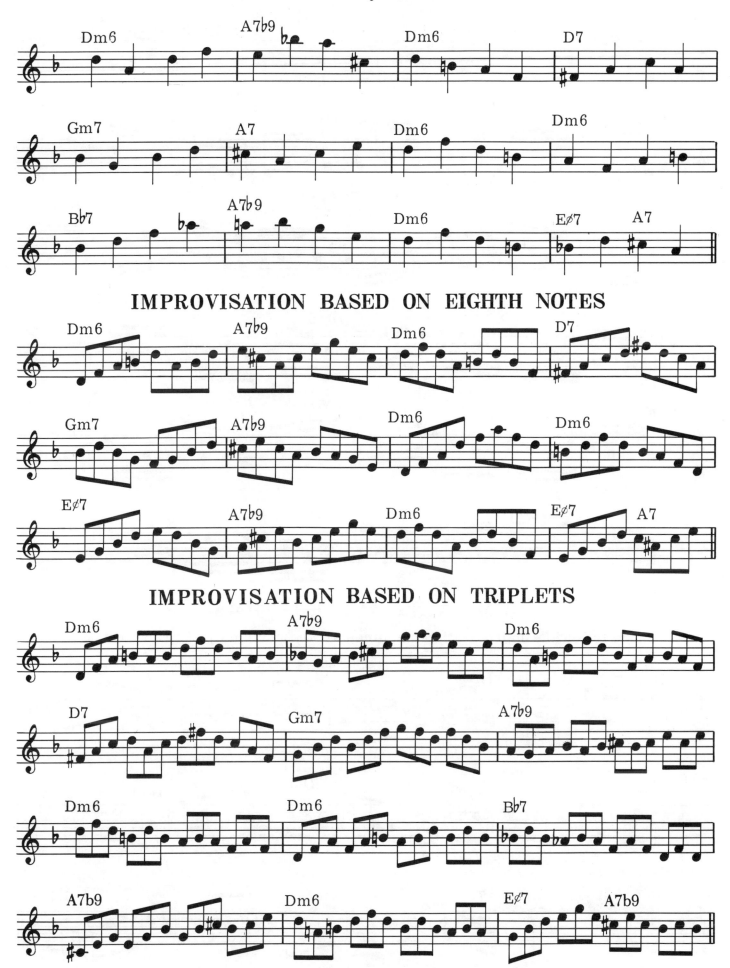

IMPROVISATION BASED ON EIGHTH NOTES

IMPROVISATION BASED ON TRIPLETS

IMPROVISATION BASED ON SIXTEENTH NOTES

COMBINING ALL RHYTHMS

The following improvisation combines all the rhythms just practiced.

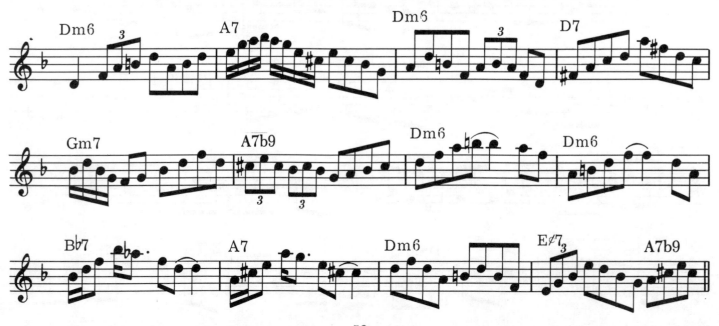

MINOR BLUES
IMPROVISING SCALES

Since the chords used in the minor blues progression are derived from the various minor scale forms and do not fit into just one minor mode, it follows that there are a number of scales which may be used for improvising against each chord. The following table lists the various scale choices in each measure of the blues progression. Notice that in the first measure since there are a number of tonic (I chord) chord possibilities there are many scale choices particularly if the chord being played is a minor triad. The progression shown is in the D minor mode.

MEAS.	CHORD	SCALE CHOICES
1.	Dm	D natural minor, D harmonic minor, D jazz minor, D dorian, D blues scale.
	Dm6	D jazz minor
	Dm7	D dorian, D natural minor
	Dm♯7	D jazz minor, D harmonic minor.
2.	A7♭9	D harmonic minor, A blues scale.
3.	SAME AS MEASURE 1.	
4.	D7	D mixolydian, D blues scale.
5.	Gm7	G dorian, G natural minor.
6.	SAME AS MEASURE 2.	
7.	SAME AS MEASURE 1.	
8.	SAME AS MEASURE 1.	
9.	B♭7	B♭ mixolydian
10.	SAME AS MEASURE 2.	
11.	SAME AS MEASURE 1.	
12.	Eø7	E* locrian, G jazz minor (IV jazz minor)
	A7♭9	SAME AS MEASURE 2.

* For the construction of the locrian mode see page 6.

Below are the improvising scale choices for the minor blues progression as listed on page 56.

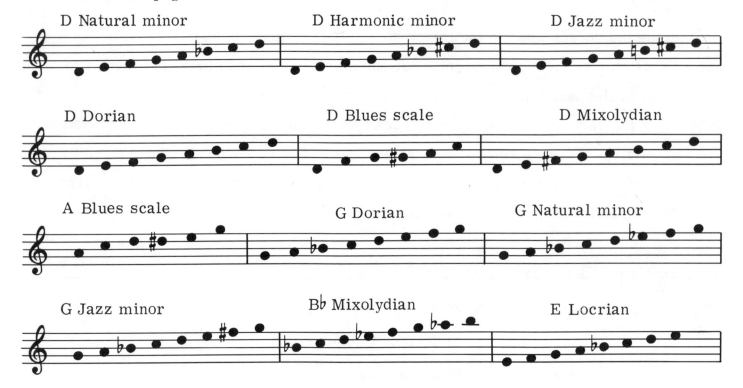

IMPROVISATION BASED ON EIGHTH NOTES

The following improvisation is based on the minor blues progression shown on page 56. All notes are taken from the scales shown above. Notice that the notes played on the 1st and 3rd beats are always a note contained in the chord. Notes occuring on the 2nd and 4th beats do not have to be a chord tone.

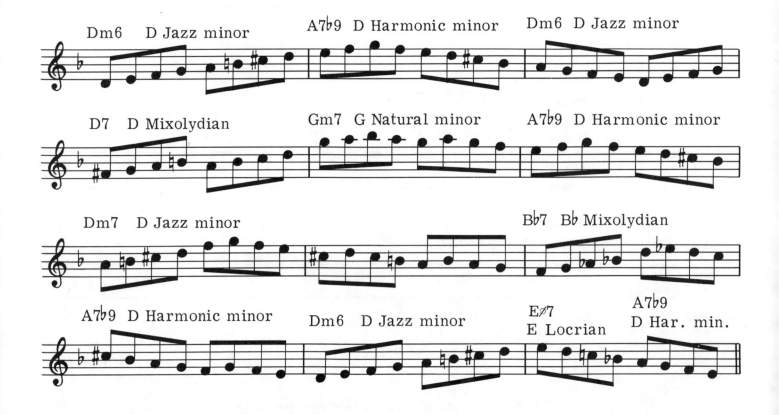

IMPROVISATION BASED ON TRIPLETS

In the following improvisation notice that the tonic minor chord (Im) is given as a Dm triad. This allows the improvisor greater leeway in determining which improvising scale to use. In this case I have chosen the D blues scale. Again notice that the notes played on the 1st and 3rd beats are chord tones.

IMPROVISATION BASED ON SIXTEENTH NOTES

MINOR BLUES SOLOS

In the following minor blues solos notice the use of the various devices we studied in earlier lessons. Sequences, repetition, lower and upper neighboring tones, motifs and a good mixture of chord and scale tones. Notice also the use of various rhythms which is so important in developing interest in a jazz solo.

SOLO NO. 1

This first solo is rhythmically simple with sequential patterns in measures 6 and 9. Notice the use of lower and upper neighboring tones in measures 6 and 9.

SOLO NO. 2

This next solo is more rhythmically complicated but the mixture of sixteenth notes and eighth notes are well balanced. There is also a good balance of chord tones and scale tones.

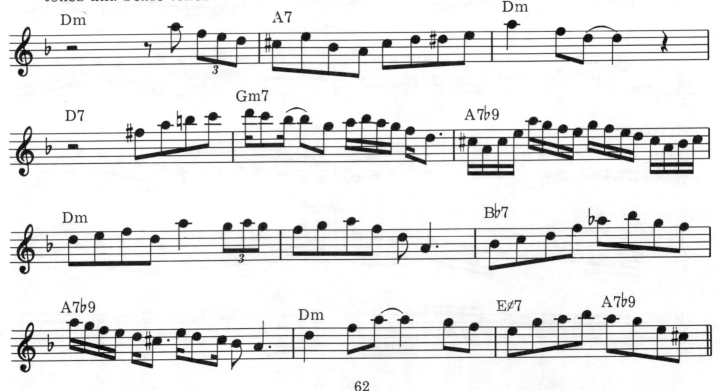

SOLO NO. 3

In this next solo the rhythm is again rather complex as in measures 5 and 11. In measures 3 and 4 their is a repetition of a rhythmic phrase. Lower and upper neighboring tones are used in measures 6 and 11 in a sequence built on chord tones. Measure 12 contains a melodic phrase repeated from the 7th of each chord.

SOLO NO. 4

Solo no. 4 is rhythmically simpler than the previous solos and makes greater use of chord tones. Notice the repetitive melodic phrase in measures 1 and 3 and again in measure 9 and 10.

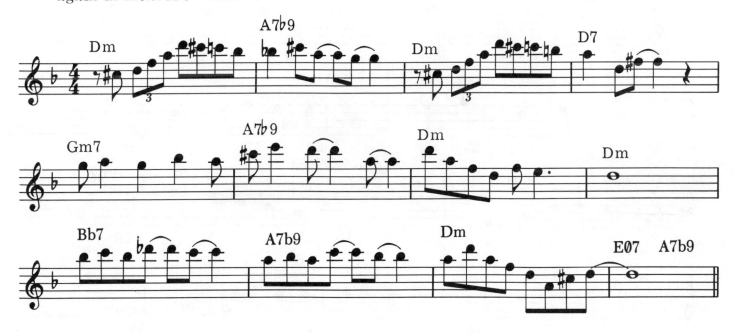

THE STANDARD POPULAR SONG

In addition to the blues another source of material for the jazz musician is
the standard popular song form. This form had its beginings in the great Broadway
musicals of the 1920's and has survived giving jazz musicians an abundance of
excellent material on which to practice their art. Below is an example of how the
form is constructed. Notice how the first two 8 measure sections are almost
identical and are labeled (A) The third 8 measure section, called the "bridge"
or the "release", is labeled (B) and the last 8 measure section is a return to
the letter (A). The chord progression is probably the most used progression by jazz musicians except for the blues. The melody is typical of so
many melodies using this form.

DREAM TIME

MELODIC EMBELLISHMENT AND FILL-INS

When jazz musicians began using the standard popular song form as a vehicle for improvisation the first solos were based on melodic embellishment. In other words the melody was the basis for the improvised solo. In those measures which contained notes of long duration short solos called "fill-ins" were used to fill out the time in place of the long note. These fill-ins were based on chord tones and passing scale tones.

Below is an example of the use of fill-ins to give our song "Dream Time" a more jazz-like flavor. Only the first sixteen measures of the song is used.

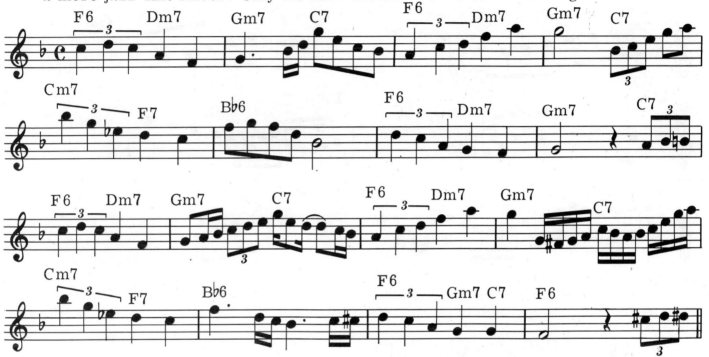

In the examples shown above the melodic flow was directed toward the first note of the next measure. In the following examples the melodic flow of the fill-ins seem suspended in mid air rather than pointed toward the first note of the next measure.

In the following example we take our melodic embellishment a step further by playing around the melody. Notice the use of lower and upper neighboring tones as well as chord and passing scale tones. Notice that the original melody may still be heard through the embellishment. Compare the examples below with the original melody on page 64.

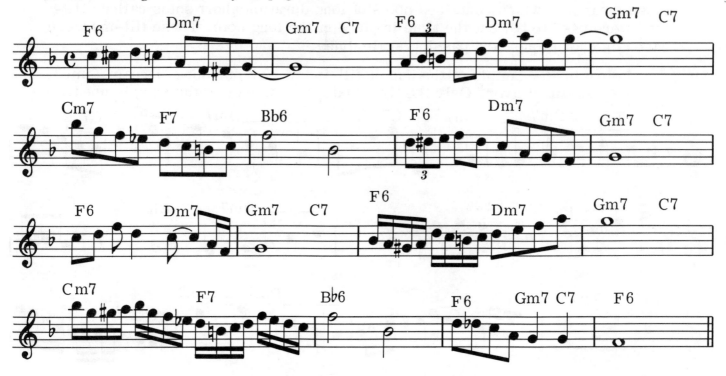

Below we see our melodic embellishment combined with the fill-ins and produces a more complete improvised solo.

66

Now having completed the first sixteen measures of improvisation around the melody of our song Dream Time, let's work on the (B) section or the bridge, of the tune.

Looking back on page 64 we find that the melody to the bridge consists of two repetitive phrases, measures 17 and 18 are repeated in measures 19 and 20. Measures 21 and 22 are repeated in measures 23 and 24. Also notice the sequence occurring between measures 17 through 20 and measures 21 through 24.

Below are three examples of possible improvisation on the melody of the bridge to our song. Notice that the patterns of repetition and sequence is retained in each example.

EXAMPLE 1. Here we make use of very simple fills in those measures.

EXAMPLE 2. Here we embellish the melody a little more. Notice the use of the upper and lower neighboring tones.

EXAMPLE 3. This last example shows that you don't have to play on every beat. Notice the long note in the last measure just waiting to bring you back to the first 8 measure section.

ELIMINATING THE MELODY

In the early 1930's jazz players began to move away from using the melody as a basis for their jazz improvisation. Players like Coleman Hawkins began to disregard the melody completely and base their solos on the chords of the tunes they were playing. Using the chords to Dream Time we see below a series of studies based strictly on the chords. Beginning with half notes and going through the various rhythms you will begin to get a feel for the chords Remember that this progression is the most commonly used progression in jazz after the blues. Notice that 1st and 2nd endings and da capo signs are used since the "A" section is repeated three times.

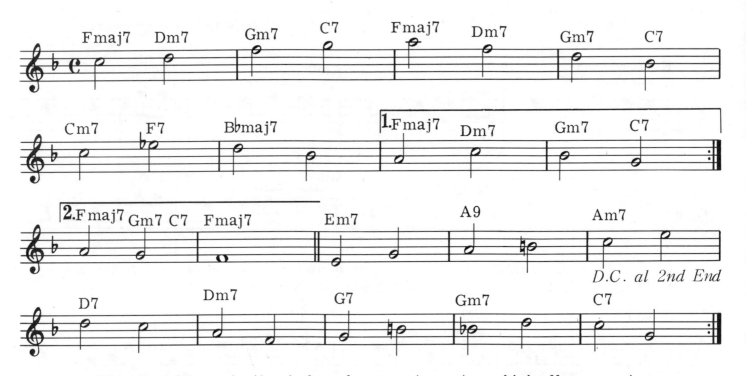

This next improvisation is based on quarter notes which allows you two notes from each chord.

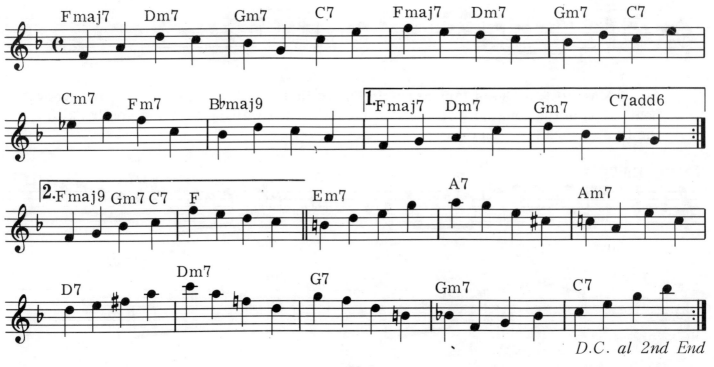

This next improvisation is based on eighth notes. Notice the increased use of 9ths and 11ths.

D.C. al 2nd End

This improvisation is based on triplets. Again, notice the greater use of 9ths and 11ths.

D.C. al 2nd End

The following improvisation is based on sixteenth notes.

The following solos are based on the chords to our song Dream Time. Notice the use of rhythm combinations and the addition of rests in order to create musical phrases. Notice also the use of lower and upper neighboring tones.

DREAM TIME IMPROVISING SCALES

Now we are going to explore some more melodic possibilities for our improvised solos by using the scalar approach. The table below lists the basic scales from which the chords to Dream Time are derived. These scales will increase our choices of notes for our solos. Later on in the book we will learn that there are many more scales which may also be used.

MEAS.	CHORD	SCALE CHOICE
1.	FMaj7 or F6	F major scale
	Dm7	F Major scale
2.	Gm7	G Dorian mode
	C7	C Mixolydian mode
3.	Same as measure 1	
4.	Same as measure 2	
5.	Cm7	C Dorian mode
	F7	F Mixolydian mode
6.	B♭ Maj7	B♭ Major scale
7.	Same as measure 1	
8.	Same as measure 2	

Measures 9 through 14 is the same as measures 1 through 6.

MEAS.	CHORD	SCALE CHOICE
15.	FMaj7	F Major scale
	Gm7	G Dorian mode
	C7	C Mixolydian mode
16.	FMaj7	F Major scale
17.	Em7	E Dorian mode
18.	A7	A Mixolydian Mode
19.	Am7	A Dorian Mode
20.	D7	D Mixolydian mode
21.	Dm7	D Dorian Mode
22.	G7	G Mixolydian Mode
23.	Gm7	G Dorian Mode
24.	C7	C Mixolydian Mode

Measures 25 through 32 are the same as measures 9 through 16.

72

Below is the musical notation of the scales shown in the table on page 72. Notice that in those measures which contain the chord FMaj7 followed by Dm7, the scale to be used throughout the entire measure is F major. The reason is that the Dm7 chord (VI chord) is often used as a substitute chord for the FMaj7. In other words the VI chord is often used as a substitute for the I chord since both chords have a large number of common tones.

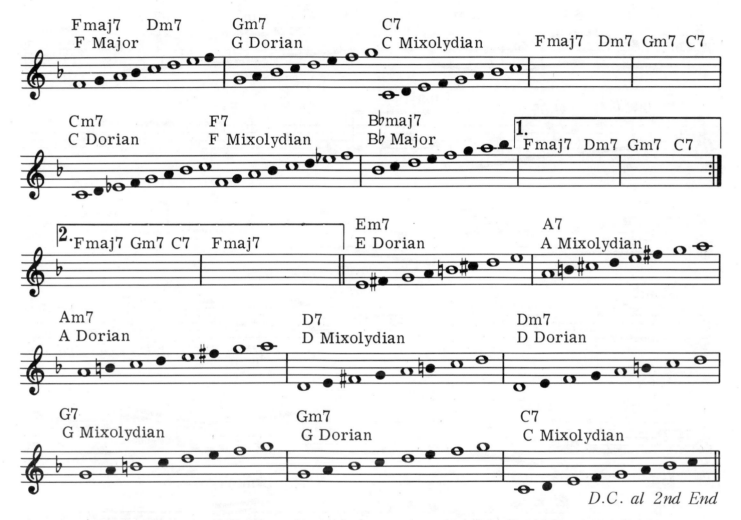

When chords are changing every two beats such as in measures 2, 4, and 5 as shown above, this often creates a problem for the soloist. One way to handle this situation is to choose a scale that can acommodate both chords. For example, in measure 2 the chords are Gm7 to C7, (II-V) since both chords are derived from the F major scale, simply play that scale through the entire measure. The same would apply to measure 4. In measure 5 the chords Cm7 to F7 are the II and V of the Bb major scale, therefore play the Bb scale through the entire measure. Another way to approach the two chords per measure situation, providing the chords are II—V in the same key, is to choose just one chord, either the II or the V and play the appropriate scale for that chord through the entire measure. For example, in measure 2 you could use either the G dorian mode or the C mixolydian mode through the entire measure. Generally speaking it's the scale for the first chord, the II chord, which is used.

The following solos illustrate a greater use of scale tones than in previous solos. To provide a proper balance you will notice that some measures make use of only chord tones. It's important that any solo not be too heavy in one direction. A good mixture of scale tones and chord tones will usually create a more interesting solo.

JAZZ SOUND-JAZZ TONE

All one has to do is just listen to any great jazz artist and almost immediately the listener will be able to identify who is playing. Unlike the classical musician who strives to produce the "ideal" sound, the jazz musician understands that individuality of sound is most important and contributes to his uniqueness. A good jazz solo is more than just playing the "correct" notes or using the melodic devices discussed earlier in the book such as motifs and repetition of phrases or sequential phrases, etc. The first thing that the listener hears is the sound or the tone of the jazz artist. Below is a brief discussion of some of the factors that contribute to the jazz players sound.

ARTICULATION

The term articulation refers to the way in which a note or a series of notes is played. Below are three marks which will illustrate the different ways in which notes may be played.

> The note is accented and held for its full value.

∧ The note is accented and played short.

— The note is attacked with a legato tongue and held for full value.

Besides the various ways in which notes are played the jazz artists also makes use of various slurred notes. In the course of his solo he mixes up certain slurred notes with certain tongued notes. Below are several examples of slurred and tongued notes along with the markings shown above.

VIBRATO

The vibrato is the pulsating effect produced by the alternation of a given tone. This is probably the most identifiable sound of any musician, Who could mistake the wide, quick vibrations of the trumpet of louis Armstrong or so many jazz artists of the swing era of the 1930's or the very slight vibrato used by Miles Davis and so many musicians of the bebop era of the 1940's. Some musicians use vibrato for almost the full value of a note and some vibrate just as the note is about to end.

Vibrato of swing era   Vibrato of bebop era

DYNAMICS

Dynamics refers to the varying degrees of softness or loudness which can add interest to a melodic line. The proper use of dynamics can make even a somewhat dull solo more interesting.

SPECIAL EFFECTS

Other ways in which a musician can develop his "own" sound is by the use of such devices as mutes for brass players. Different mutes produce different kinds of sounds. The use of alternate fingerings for a particular note may create an interesting effect when the note is first played with its original fingering and then played with its alternate fingering. Lester Young the tenor saxophonist with Count Basie was well known for that. The use of the glissando which is the sliding effect created by literaly sliding the fingers off the keys when going from a low note to a higher note. On a string instrument the glissando is produced by sliding the finger along the string. Clarinet and sax players can produce a very soft sound called sub-tone, almost like a breathy effect which is quite effective on slow songs. The bending upward of strings on a stringed instrument creates a "bluesey" effect and is used a great deal by blues players. Different kinds of mouthpieces produce different sounds. It's important that a wind instrument player try out many kinds of mouthpieces in order to hear the different sounds that are available to him. Players of valved instruments can make interesting use of half valve notes. Smears, which is a way of approaching a note from another note slightly below the main note, is another very characteristic sound of many jazz players. It's a short glissando or slide from the lower note to the main note. Ghost notes too are heard in many jazz solos. These are notes that are fingered but are barely heard so that the true pitch is hardly discernable.

TENSION AND RELEASE - MELODICALLY

One of the important ingredients of a good jazz solo is a principle called tension and release. Tension and release is inherent in all the three elements of music, melody (scales) harmony (chords) and rhythm. Since a jazz solo is a melody based on chords we will combine melody and harmony and see how this principle of tension and release works to create a more interesting jazz solo.

Below are examples of tension and release which occurs whenever a V7 chord is followed by a I chord.

Notice in the examples above how the tension generated by the notes within the G7 chord is released as soon as we reach the C chord. Notice also how the G7 wants to move toward the C chord creating a foward motion. From the above observations we can conclude that the greater the tension, the more satisfying the release. Also, the greater the tension the greater the desire to move forward and a jazz solo should always have a sense of going forward.

CREATING GREATER TENSION

One of the ways to introduce greater tension in a jazz solo is to extend the notes of the chords. See page 37. Since we are concerning ourselves with the V7 chord (the dominant chords) let's extend the G7 chord and see the tension notes.

Another way to introduce greater tension in the V7 chord is to alter certain notes within the chord. Since these altered notes are foreign to the key which the V7 belongs to the tension produced by these altered notes is very great and demands resolution or release by the I chord. Below are the altered notes of the G7 with its extensions.

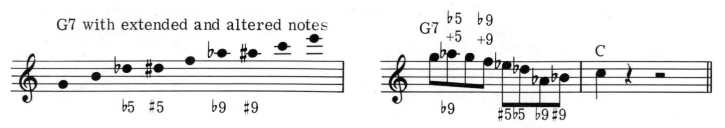

77

CONTROLLING TENSION

It's important to understand that it isn't necessary to use all of the altered notes in your jazz solo. You may use as many or as few as your taste dictates. Also it isn't necessary to relearn every dominant 7th (V7) chord with each of its altered notes. In the mid 1960's jazz artists like John Coltarne began experimenting with the use of various scales which could be played over a dominant 7th chord and will automatically contain all of the altered notes of that chord. One of the most commonly used scales is the jazz minor scale. See page 55. The jazz minor scale contains all of the altered notes for any dominant 7th chord whose root is a half step BELOW the tonic note of the scale. In other words to find the correct jazz minor scale for any domiant 7th chord simply use the scale whose tonic note is a half step higher than the root of the chord. For example, for the G7 chord use the Ab jazz minor scale.

Below is the Ab jazz minor scale showing how its notes are related to the G7.

Ab Jazz Minor

| G7 | b9 | #9 | 3 | b5 | #5 | 7 | R | b9 |

A simple way of learning the various jazz minor scales is to think of the major scale and flat the 3rd of the major scale, the result will be a jazz minor scale. Below is a comparrison between the Ab major scale and the Ab jazz minor scale.

Ab Major

Flatting the 3rd produces the Ab
Jazz Minor

(b3)

The following examples illustrate the use of the Ab jazz minor scale resolving to the C chord. The actual progression would be G7-C. In the first several examples the altered notes are included in the chord symbol only to help you in analysing the melodic line. Normally it is not necessary to include the alterations in the chord symbol. The choice of which notes to alter are left strictly to the improvisor. However, if the composer or the arranger definitely wants certain notes to be altered then he will indicate it in the chord symbol and the improvisor then must include them in his solo.

A very effective method of controlling the amount of tension in an improvised solo is through the use of various scales which contain those altered notes that create the desired tension. You have just seen how the jazz minor scale may be used to create four altered notes of a dominant 7th chord. Now let's examine some other scales which may also produce varying amounts of tension.

LYDIAN-DOMINANT SCALE

The lydian - dominant scale, also called the lydian ♭7 scale, may be used with a dominant 7th chord with a ♯11th (or a ♭5th). Below is the G lydian-dominant scale and its relationship to the G7 chord.

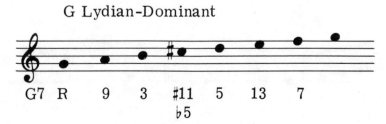

G Lydian-Dominant

G7	R	9	3	♯11	5	13	7
				♭5			

NOTICE: Another way of thinking of the above scale is to call it a G mixolydian with the 4th note raised a half step.

Below are several examples of the G lydian-dominant scale resolving to the C chord.

ALTERED DOMINANT SCALE

Below is an altered-dominant 7 scale which contains the ♭9 of the dominant 7th chord. The scale may also be used for any dominant 7 chord which calls for a ♭9 in the chord symbol Ex. C7♭9, the G altered-dominant scale is shown with its relationship to the G7 chord.

G Altered - Dominant

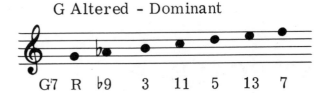

G7 R ♭9 3 11 5 13 7

NOTICE: Another way of thinking of the scale is to think of the G mixolydian with the 2nd note flatted a half step.

Below are several examples of the G altered-dominant scale resolving to the C chord.

DIMINISHED SCALE WHOLE STEP-HALF STEP

Another scale which offers the improvisor a number of possible tension notes is the diminished scale. The diminished scale is derived from the diminished seventh chord.

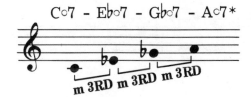

The diminished seventh chord is constructed of successive minor thirds and because of its symmetrical construction any of the notes in the chord may be considered the root.

The diminished scale is constructed in alternating WHOLE STEPS and HALP STEPS. Like the diminished seventh chord the scale also has four possible tonic notes.

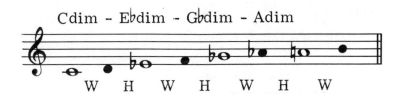

The diminished scale is obviously best when applied to the diminished seventh chord when improvising, however, for our immediate purposes in using scales to create tension, the diminished scale is frequently applied to the dominant 7th chord. The correct diminished scale to use is the scale whose tonic note is a HALF-STEP higher than the dominant 7th chord. In other words, for a G7 chord use an A♭ diminished scale. See the relationship below.

Below are several examples of the A♭ diminished scale applied to the G7 chord resolving to the C chord

*Notice that the note "A" is the enharmonic equivalent of the B♭♭ which would be the correct notation. The B♭♭ is too awkward so the "A" is used instead.

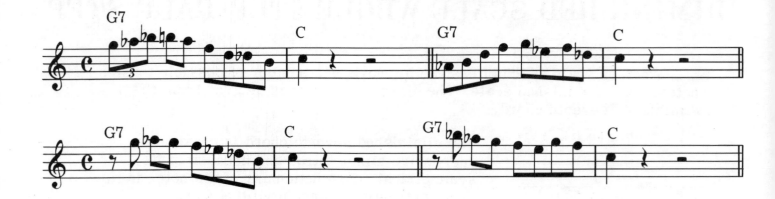

WHOLE TONE SCALE

The whole tone scale is constructed of a succession of whole steps. Since each of the notes are equi-distant from each other, any of the notes may be thought of as the letter-name of the scale.

C Whole tone scale

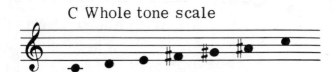

The whole tone scale is used with the dominant 7th chord and produces the tension notes ♯5 and ♭5. The scale is also used when the chord symbol indicates those notes. Ex. G7+5 or G7♭5. See below for the scale and its relationship to the G7 chord.

G Whole tone

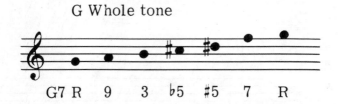

| G7 | R | 9 | 3 | ♭5 | ♯5 | 7 | R |

Below are several examples of G whole tone scale applied to the G7 chord.

PENTATONIC SCALES

Another device for controlling the amount of tension in an improvised solo is through the use of pentatonic scales. A pentatonic scale is constructed from the 1st, 2nd, 3rd, 5th, and 6th notes of the major scale.

Below are all the pentatonic scales based on every major scale.

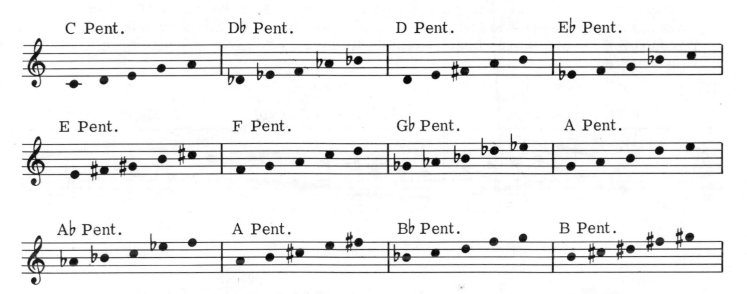

In order to determine how many tension notes each pentatonic scale will produce, go through each scale and beneath each note of the scale write in the numbered relationship to whichever chord you are working on. For example, in order to find some good scales to play against a G7 chord choose several of the penatonic scales and write out the numbered relationship to the G7 chord See Below.

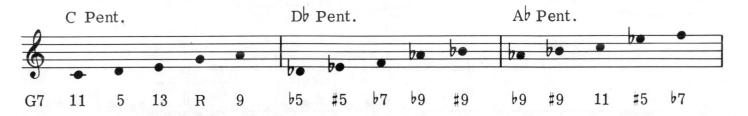

| G7 | 11 | 5 | 13 | R | 9 | ♭5 | ♯5 | ♭7 | ♭9 | ♯9 | ♭9 | ♯9 | 11 | ♯5 | ♭7 |

Notice that the C pentatonic offers the 11th, 5th, 13th, root, and 9th. All the notes except the 11th are good against the G7 but offer very little in the way of tension. The 11th is not good since the 11th sounds best when it is raised. The D♭ pentatonic offers the ♭5, ♯5, ♭9, and ♯9 so the D♭ pentatonic is a good scale to play against the G7 chord. The A♭ pentatonic is good but don't linger on the note C. You should go through all the dominant 7th chords in the same way.

The minor 7th may also take some tension notes and so you should experiment again with the various pentatonic scales. Your ear is the best judge of what "works" and what doesn't.

The Major 7th chord usually is used with the ♯11 and in recent years the ♯5 has also been used more frequently.

DREAM TIME SOLO 1.

One of the best ways to learn how to use any new scale is to use it often and in many different harmonic patterns, in that way your fingers will become accustomed to the scale and your ear will tell you when it sounds best and in what kind of pattern. The following examples are based on the harmonic background to Dream Time and each example illustrates some of the scales we have just studied.

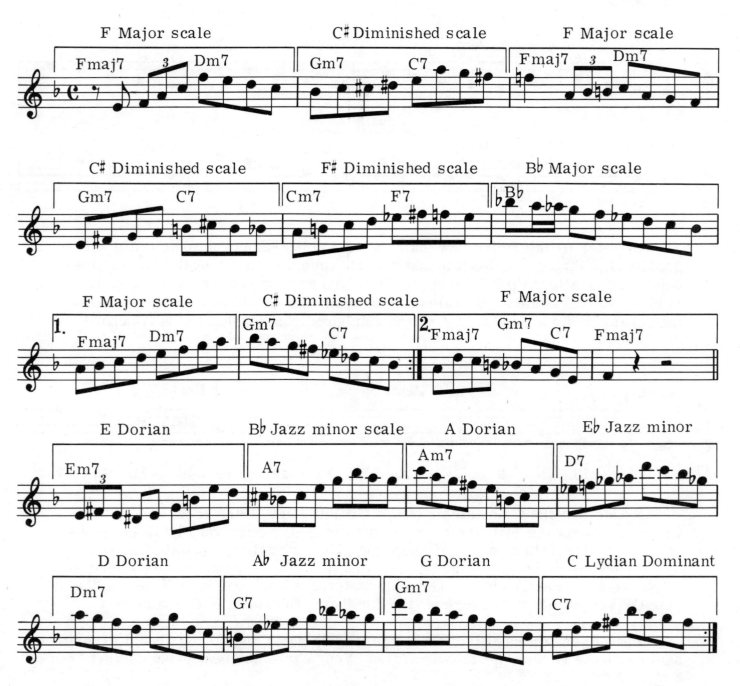

NOTE: The above scale choices are not necessarily the best choices but do show what could be used. Too much tension caused altered scales have a tendency to destroy the sense of tonality and is not recommended. There is no substitution for good taste.

DREAM TIME SOLO 2.

The following example illustrates the use of the pentatonic scales for the first sixteen measures of the tune, the "B" section of the tune. The bridge makes use of the jazz minor scales but differently than in the previous example. When the dominant 7th chords do not resolve to the tonic chords then use the jazz minor built from the 5th of the dominant chord. For example, when the G7 does not resolve to the C chord you play the D jazz minor scale. Notice that the D minor is the II of the Dm7-G7 progression therefore use the D jazz minor for the complete progression. See below.

*NOTICE: Since the C7 resolves back to the F major 7 chord in the first measure the scale used is the jazz minor built a half step higher than the root of the C7, the C♯ jazz minor.

TENSION AND RELEASE
(RHYTHMICALLY)

In learning how to develop a good jazz solo one must be aware that every bit as important and maybe even more important than the notes being played is the rhythm factor. The beats that the notes are being played on. Tension may be produced rhythmically as well as melodically. Any good jazz solo has to have a feeling of going foward just as reading a good story which keeps you looking foward to the next page or paragraph to find out what's going to happen. Up to now we have examined some of the things that you can do melodically to create tension and resolution and we learned about a number of different scales which may be used to create tension. Obviously there are many more scales that are beyond the scope of this book but may be found in a number of other books on scales. At this point I want to examine some of the ways in which rhythm may be used to create tension and release.

Below is two measures of quarter notes played in 4/4 time. There is a natural tendency in music to place greater emphasis or accent on the 1st and 3rd beats as shown by the accent marks. Also shown is two measures containing 8th notes with the natural accents coming on the downbeats.

Now if we consider that the 1st and 3rd beats of the measure are points of resolution then the 2nd and 4th beats may be thought of as points of tension. In order to create interest in a jazz solo, in order to create the feeling of moving forward, then we should have more phrases starting on the points of tension and ending on the points of release so that we have a pattern of tension-release, tension - release. This moves the solo foward. Not resolution-tension, resolution-tension. That keeps the solo from going anyplace. Upbeats are also tension notes and downbeats are release notes so more phrases should begin on upbeats. Play the following examples.

Original solo   Variation 1.

Variation 2.   Variation 3.

Below is a four bar solo based on all eighth notes. Following that is several examples of the same solo but with certain phrases starting on upbeats and certain phrases coming on downbeats.

It's also important to arrive at a release note on the 1st or 3rd beats because those beats offer release of tension. We can hear that in a simple "C" scale.

Notice how we arrive at the release note "C" too soon

Hear how the release note "C" sounds better played on the downbeat.

Release

The following rhythm patterns are good examples of tension and release and should be memorized and incorporated into your solos.

CONCLUSION

At this point I'd like to say some parting words on what you may do to improve your ability to create good jazz solos. Probably the best way to help yourself is to get a collection of some of the best solos you can get on recordings. Practice singing along with any solo of your chouce. Try to sing as accurately as possible. Breathe where the soloist breathes, get every inflection. First sing with the record then sing the solo away from the record. When you can sing the solo perfectly then try to play the solo on your instrument as close to the original as you possibly can. Do this for a dozen or more solos and this will help you immeasurably. Try to get the same feeling as the original soloist on the recording. There are many fine books that may be bought which contain transcribed solos which are also excellent for studying and comparing the notes against the given chord symbols. There are also many books that contain scales not included in this book. These scales will help in your choice of notes however a word of caution, knowing more and more scales does not make you a better jazz player. If you can't play pretty, interesting solos with the scales given in this book then knowing anymore scales will not make you more creative. Having a fine vocabulary doesn't necessarily make a person a more profound speaker. A man with a limited vocabulary can very often speak great words of wisdom. I wish you lots of luck and remember "straight ahead".